THE LAUNDRY LISTS WORKBOOK

WORKBOOK

Integrating Our Laundry Lists Traits

THE LAUNDRY LISTS WORKBOOK

Integrating Our Laundry Lists Traits

Adult Children of Alcoholics®/Dysfunctional Families
World Service Organization
Post Office Box 811
Lakewood, CA 90714-0811
www.adultchildren.org

—

The Laundry Lists Workbook
Integrating Our Laundry Lists Traits

ISBN 978-0-9965049-1-1

—

Printed in the United States of America

9 10 11   22 21 20 19

Contents

FOREWORD

*W*hen the ACA Fellowship Text was being reviewed, a copy was sent to a member who thought the book was great, except that it did not mention how we "act out"[1] **The Laundry List** effects. While the original Laundry List describes how we were affected by alcoholism and family dysfunction, the member pointed out that as adults, we might, in turn, "act out" those traits by becoming victimizers. In other words, adult children, by adopting their parents' behaviors, "become" their parents. That simple observation planted the seed for the development of **The Other Laundry List** and provides a fuller picture of how we are affected by the effects of alcoholism and family dysfunction.

The Other Laundry List is briefly mentioned in the *ACA Fellowship Text* (BRB pp. 8-9), and a fuller explanation was presented at a convention in 2008. In addition, **The Flip Side of The Laundry List** and **The Flip Side of The Other Laundry List** were presented, detailing how, through reparenting and practicing the ACA Twelve Steps, we might be freed from these effects.

The "Complete Picture" schematic preceding Appendix A provides a detailed landscape of all the areas we may travel on our journey to achieve wholeness. Taken together, the schematic and *The Laundry Lists Workbook* describe how dissociation[2] may appear in adult children. Following are reflections on the Laundry Lists Traits. A fuller explanation of dissociation as a "game" or script[3] appears on p. 155.

Please note that this workbook is for ACAs who are ready to embark on advanced work on their survival traits. It is designed for ACAs who have already gone through all the Steps in the ACA *Twelve Steps Workbook*. Since the nature of integrating our laundry lists traits can be quite involved, we suggest the use of a separate notebook for recording in-depth reflections, journaling, and for exploring non-dominant handwriting.

Some adult children also may meet informally to work through *The Laundry Lists Workbook*. These groups should adhere to the principles and traditions of ACA groups. Each participant should agree to practice honesty and courtesy, in addition to helping keep the group safe. The principle of anonymity should be honored as well.

---

1 The term "acting out" is used by mental health professionals to denote that someone has a subconscious conflict that they "act out".

2 The term "dissociation" refers to a mechanism that allows the mind to separate or compartmentalize certain memories or thoughts from normal consciousness. These split-off mental contents are not erased. They may resurface spontaneously or be triggered by objects or events in the person's environment. Additional terms used by mental health professionals include "learned dissociation", "continuum of dissociation", and "involuntary dissociation".

3 The "game" model of social interaction was introduced by Dr. Eric Berne as a social patterning function, with "games" being identified as behavioral "scripts" enacted by individuals in attempts to manipulate a social situation. For an example of how the "Game" of Dissociation is acted out in a dysfunctional family setting, see p. 155.

Acknowledgments

Our most heartfelt gratitude and appreciation goes to the support and involvement of the ACA fellowship – to those adult children, groups, and Intergroups who gave of their time to seriously review, discuss, and reflect on the content and who provided valuable commentary and suggestions for expansion and improvement. Your caring, concern, and willingness to share and express your views are truly inspiring.

Finally, this book could not have happened without the spiritual guidance of our Higher Power.

From a space of love, we give service in ACA so that every adult child seeking recovery may find a safe place.

Dedication

This book is dedicated to adult children who seek to find new levels of clarity – to those who have been guided by their Higher Power to open the pages of this book to explore an even deeper understanding of their True Selves on their spiritual journey.

From a space of love, we give service in ACA so that every adult child seeking recovery may find a safe place.

Orientation

Please consider having something on hand to use to engage all of your senses – sight, sound, taste, smell, and feel – to make sure you are present while using this book. Following are some suggestions:

Look at some things (actual)
Make a noise
Eat a peach
Smell some cinnamon
Pat your face

The point is to have *something* on hand to remind yourself that you are in the *here and now* while engaging in these tasks. Above all, be gentle with yourself when using this book.

After you have written your reflections, in order to be assured that the work was done in an integrative and nurturing manner, you may ask, "Do any of my responses seem critical?" If so, then you may want to consider revisiting those questions.

You may also check in and ask, "How does my Inner Child feel about these responses?" and continue to process what comes up for you.

THE COMPLETE PICTURE
Characteristics of an Adult Child

The Laundry List

1) We became isolated and afraid of people and authority figures.

2) We became approval seekers and lost our identity in the process.

3) We are frightened by angry people and any personal criticism.

4) We either become alcoholics, marry them or both, or find another compulsive personality such as a workaholic to fulfill our sick abandonment needs.

5) We live life from the viewpoint of victims and we are attracted by that weakness in our love and friendship relationships.

6) We have an overdeveloped sense of responsibility and it is easier for us to be concerned with others rather than ourselves. This enables us not to look too closely at our own faults.

7) We get guilt feelings when we stand up for ourselves instead of giving in to others.

8) We become addicted to excitement.

9) We confuse love with pity and tend to "love" people who we can "pity" and "rescue".

10) We have stuffed our feelings from our traumatic childhoods and have lost the ability to feel or express our feelings because it hurts so much (denial).

11) We judge ourselves harshly and have a very low sense of self-esteem.

12) We are dependent personalities who are terrified of abandonment and will do anything to hold on to a relationship in order not to experience painful abandonment feelings which we received from living with sick people who were never there emotionally for us.

13) Alcoholism is a family disease and we became para-alcoholics and took on the characteristics of the disease even though we did not pick up the drink.

14) Para-alcoholics are reactors rather than actors.

Victim / Rescuer I

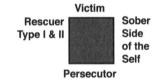

Unintegrated and

In the "Game" of Dissociation these positions are receivers of insult & injury* delivered by dissociative dosing transactions.

Completing the Cycle of Violence
Closing the Circle
Positions in The Game of Dissociation

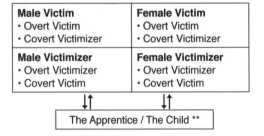

Male Victim	Female Victim
• Overt Victim	• Overt Victim
• Covert Victimizer	• Covert Victimizer
Male Victimizer	**Female Victimizer**
• Overt Victimizer	• Overt Victimizer
• Covert Victim	• Covert Victim

The Apprentice / The Child **

Bringing the Family Drama to a Close
(Withdrawing from The Game of Dissociation)

Persecutor   Rescuer Type I & II

Victim

The Drama Triangle*

Victim

Rescuer Type I & II   Sober Side of the Self

Persecutor

A Fourth Possibility

Characteristics of an Integrated Person

The Flip Side of The Laundry List

1) We move out of isolation and are not unrealistically afraid of other people, even authority figures.

2) We do not depend on others to tell us who we are.

3) We are not automatically frightened by angry people and no longer regard personal criticism as a threat.

4) We do not have a compulsive need to recreate abandonment.

5) We stop living life from the standpoint of victims and are not attracted by this trait in our important relationships.

6) We do not use enabling as a way to avoid looking at our own shortcomings.

7) We do not feel guilty when we stand up for ourselves.

8) We avoid emotional intoxication and choose workable relationships instead of constant upset.

9) We are able to distinguish love from pity, and do not think "rescuing" people we "pity" is an act of love.

10) We come out of denial about our traumatic childhoods and regain the ability to feel and express our emotions.

11) We stop judging and condemning ourselves and discover a sense of self-worth.

12) We grow in independence and are no longer terrified of abandonment. We have interdependent relationships with healthy people, not dependent relationships with people who are emotionally unavailable.

13) The characteristics of alcoholism and para-alcoholism we have internalized are identified, acknowledged, and removed.

14) We are actors, not reactors.

---

*   Note: Insult and Injury = Punishment, abandonment, conditional acceptance, conditional care

** "Oh, No! These are my choices?"

*** Following Karpman 1967, 2007

For an explanation of the roles and transactions in the "Game" of Dissociation, see p. 155.

The Other Laundry List / The Opposite Laundry List
(A reaction Formation List; "It Will Never Happen To Me")

1) To cover our fear of people and our dread of isolation we tragically become the very authority figures who frighten others and cause them to withdraw.
2) To avoid becoming enmeshed and entangled with other people and losing ourselves in the process, we become rigidly self-sufficient. We disdain the approval of others.
3) We frighten people with our anger and threat of belittling criticism.
4) We dominate others and abandon them before they can abandon us or we avoid relationships with dependent people altogether. To avoid being hurt, we isolate and dissociate and thereby abandon ourselves.
5) We live life from the standpoint of a victimizer, and are attracted to people we can manipulate and control in our important relationships.
6) We are irresponsible and self-centered. Our inflated sense of self-worth and self-importance prevents us from seeing our deficiencies and shortcomings.
7) We make others feel guilty when they attempt to assert themselves.
8) We inhibit our fear by staying deadened and numb.
9) We hate people who "play" the victim and beg to be rescued.
10) We deny that we've been hurt and are suppressing our emotions by the dramatic expression of "pseudo" feelings.
11) To protect ourselves from self punishment for failing to "save" the family we project our self-hate onto others and punish them instead.
12) We "manage" the massive amount of deprivation we feel, coming from abandonment within the home, by quickly letting go of relationships that threaten our "independence" (not too close).
13) We refuse to admit we've been affected by family dysfunction or that there was dysfunction in the home or that we have internalized any of the family's destructive attitudes and behaviors.
14) We act as if we are nothing like the dependent people who raised us.

---

emotionally intoxicated

Rescuer II / Persecutor

In the "Game" of Dissociation these positions are givers of insult & injury* delivered by dissociative dosing transactions.

Completing the Recovery Process

Victim
Rescuer Type I & II
Persecutor
Sober Side of the Self

→

Whole, healthy, sane & safe

The Sober Self

The Flip Side of The Other Laundry List

1) We face and resolve our fear of people and our dread of isolation and stop intimidating others with our power and position.
2) We realize the sanctuary we have built to protect the frightened and injured child within has become a prison and we become willing to risk moving out of isolation.
3) With our renewed sense of self-worth and self-esteem we realize it is no longer necessary to protect ourselves by intimidating others with contempt, ridicule and anger.
4) We accept and comfort the isolated and hurt inner child we have abandoned and disavowed and thereby end the need to act out our fears of enmeshment and abandonment with other people.
5) Because we are whole and complete we no longer try to control others through manipulation and force and bind them to us with fear in order to avoid feeling isolated and alone.
6) Through our in-depth inventory we discover our true identity as capable, worthwhile people. By asking to have our shortcomings removed we are freed from the burden of inferiority and grandiosity.
7) We support and encourage others in their efforts to be assertive.
8) We uncover, acknowledge and express our childhood fears and withdraw from emotional intoxication.
9) We have compassion for anyone who is trapped in the "drama triangle" and is desperately searching for a way out of insanity.
10) We accept we were traumatized in childhood and lost the ability to feel. Using the 12 Steps as a program of recovery we regain the ability to feel and remember and become whole human beings who are happy, joyous and free.
11) In accepting we were powerless as children to "save" our family we are able to release our self-hate and to stop punishing ourselves and others for not being enough.
12) By accepting and reuniting with the inner child we are no longer threatened by intimacy, by the fear of being engulfed or made invisible.
13) By acknowledging the reality of family dysfunction we no longer have to act as if nothing were wrong or keep denying that we are still unconsciously reacting to childhood harm and injury.
14) We stop denying and do something about our post-traumatic dependency on substances, people, places and things to distort and avoid reality.

TRAIT
ONE

Trait 1

The Laundry List	The Other Laundry List
We became isolated and afraid of people and authority figures.	*To cover our fear of people and our dread of isolation we tragically become the very authority figures who frighten others and cause them to withdraw.*
The Flip Side of The Laundry List	**The Flip Side of The Other Laundry List**
We move out of isolation and are not unrealistically afraid of other people, even authority figures.	*We face and resolve our fear of people and our dread of isolation and stop intimidating others with our power and position.*

Our families were not safe enough for us to feel comfortable in being ourselves. Thus, we isolated ourselves by burying, hiding, denying, abandoning, and betraying our True Self and presenting a false self to the world. From this protective space, we could keep our fear of people at an acceptable level. We didn't allow many folks the opportunity to hurt us, and when they were able to get close, any separation produced an almost intolerable feeling of pain that led us to refortify our defenses and to further isolate ourselves from any intimacy. The same scenario was played out with authority figures either at work or at play. Our rebelliousness *to authority* was more an acting out of this trait than any legitimate push back *against authority*.

In this process of dissociation we had mastered the moves: isolate ourselves and continue to fear people and authority. Combined with the inevitable separation, we experience even deeper pain, greater isolation, and more fear. Game, set, and match! On it goes until we hit bottom and become willing to admit that we are powerless over this effect and that our lives had become unmanageable. We had dissociated from ourselves and others so perfectly that we felt we had mastered the process of dissociation. This process only produces a constant downward spiral of increasing loneliness and exaggerated fear that cripples our ability to engage in meaningful relationships or to be productive members of our society.

Still, the childhood loss of trust permeates all of our interactions, relationships, and intimacy as the repetition or recycling of our traumatic childhood dynamics beckons us to find resolution or expression of our original pain. This is a natural and logical response to the chaotic family dynamics we were raised in as described in **The Laundry List**.

However, many ACAs seem to have overcome their fear of people and authority figures, and it is presumed that we have achieved – despite our upbringing – a measure of success due to our resilience. Some of us understandably occupy positions of relative authority. Some of us may even occupy seats of power in corporations and nations. In a real sense, our childhood experiences made us adept at maintaining control, multi-tasking, managing chaos, and being decisive – all useful qualities for those in a position of authority.

On the other hand, maintaining control, multi-tasking, managing chaos, and being decisive were also dissociating skills, which we learned to make our childhoods safe. This dissociation may also reflect a form of acting out. We become the very authority figures who frighten others and cause them to withdraw.

Outwardly, we may be socially celebrated and well respected, but this is an ironic validation of our false self. The cost of this "success" for our "leadership" is that we may still be unconsciously reacting to our childhood dynamics – still being a hero or martyr. The payoff for our acting out in this manner is that we are actually "denying" our True Self and reinforcing our overly protective and defensive false self. To maintain this "false authority" self, we unconsciously dose ourselves with adrenaline to feed constant fear, anger, or pain to armor ourselves against our unrealistic fear of people and the dread of being isolated, as described in **The Other Laundry List**.

Thus dissociated, we are compelled to continue to sacrifice our True Self so that we do not lose our false sense of security through the dysfunctional family tactics of people pleaser, problem solver, quick thinker, or decision maker. Controlling or manipulating takes the place of genuine living.

From this protective and domineering position, we can often unknowingly and sometimes purposely intimidate our family members, friends, subordinates, and superiors. We can cause them to obey us with little regard to their humanness, figuring that the supposed skills we have developed are better than any actual weakness the people we deal with may have.

With the consistent daily work we do in ACA, we move out of isolation and are not unrealistically afraid of other people, even authority figures (**The Flip Side of The Laundry List**). When confronted by adult situations, we can learn not to regress to a stage in our childhood. We can respond appropriately to the situation at hand. Freeing ourselves from the childhood reactions of isolating and extraordinary fear, we can reparent ourselves, take the ACA Twelve Steps, get clear about how the effect is impacting us, and decide to try a different approach.

When challenged about our positions of power (**The Other Laundry List**), we can face and resolve our fear of people and our dread of isolation, and stop intimidating others with our power and position (**The Flip Side of The Other Laundry List**). No longer driven by unconscious fear of people and dread of being alone, we can engage *with* the world, accepting the demands of our position while not depriving family members, friends, or our colleagues of their dignity and integrity. This will take a great deal of effort on our part, and we may not be able to immediately recognize how this effect drives us to be reactionary or how it impacts those around us. The meetings and our fellow travelers may help us if we ask. The effect on us and those around us will gradually become clearer as we develop the insight and experience garnered from working the ACA Steps and reparenting ourselves, one day at a time. The gifts of becoming a whole, integrated human being will make the journey of life a wonderful adventure with the ever-present guide of our Higher Power, without whom these gifts may go unrealized. (**The Flip Side of The Other Laundry List**)

ORIENTATION
Be Prepared to Engage Your Senses

Look at some things (actual)
Make a noise
Eat a peach
Smell some cinnamon
Pat your face

Trait 1 Reflections

The Laundry List
We became isolated and afraid of people and authority figures.

1. When have I been isolated and afraid of people and authority figures?

2. Where and when has this occurred?

3. How does my body react when I am in fear?

4. What do I do to help my body come back to a calm inner state?

5. Has isolation become almost comfortable? If so, how?

6. List all the people or types of people who you perceive today as authority figures.

7. This trait says "we became afraid of people". Who have you been afraid of in the past and who are you afraid of now? This might be certain people with names or it might be types of people.

The Other Laundry List

To cover our fear of people and our dread of isolation we tragically become the very authority figures who frighten others and cause them to withdraw.

1. How do I cover my fear of people?

2. What situations in my life cause me to dread isolation?

3. When have I been an authority figure who frightens or intimidates others?

4. When I am acting as an authority figure, who have I caused to withdraw?

5. Who dominated or intimidated me when I was a child?

6. What have I done to purposely frighten or dominate a person?

7. Describe a relationship in detail you've been involved in where one person dominated.

The Flip Side of The Laundry List

We move out of isolation and are not unrealistically afraid of other people, even authority figures.

1. What tools have I used to move out of isolation?

2. Which ACA Steps have helped me gauge when it was appropriate to be afraid of other people, even authority figures?

3. Which people in my life do I consider an authority figure? Can these people's status change over time?

4. Since finding ACA, what phases have I gone through in coming out of isolation?

The Flip Side of The Other Laundry List

We face and resolve our fear of people and our dread of isolation and stop intimidating others with our power and position.

1. How has the ACA program helped me face and resolve my fear of people and dread of isolation?

2. What principles of the ACA program have allowed me to stop intimidating others with my power and position?

3. How do I appropriately act within my power and position without intimidating others?

4. What specific fears of people and authority figures have lessened for me?

5. Are there people who are realistically fearsome? If so, make a list of those people or types of people and why they are on your list.

TRAIT
TWO

Trait 2

The Laundry List	The Other Laundry List
We became approval seekers and lost our identity in the process.	*To avoid becoming enmeshed and entangled with other people and losing ourselves in the process, we become rigidly self-sufficient. We disdain the approval of others.*
The Flip Side of The Laundry List	**The Flip Side of The Other Laundry List**
We do not depend on others to tell us who we are.	*We realize the sanctuary we have built to protect the frightened and injured child within has become a prison and we become willing to risk moving out of isolation.*

*C*hildren need, seek, and expect that their parents or their caregivers will approve of them. When a parent is emotionally, physically, or spiritually absent, the child learns to reverse the relationship's current flow and instead becomes the one who works to gain the approval of their caregivers by acting in the way that seems to get the caregiver's attention and love. This initiates the Game of Dissociation. Our true identities are hidden from our caregivers and, more importantly, from ourselves. Paradoxically, we lose our true identity and we lose an essential ingredient to healthy development – to be valued for who we are versus who our caregivers wanted us to be. We placate our caregivers and become an unwilling victim in the Game of Dissociation. (**The Laundry List**)

The people-pleasing false self seems like the solution to all of our problems. We are performing for people and they appear to be happy with us. The problem is that the people-pleasing false self is dishonest. We fall into despair, anger and depression, fretting over controlling the uncontrollable, our false self, and the reactions of people.

In this we are not alone. We are in a constant state of worry – trying to suppress who we are while figuring out who others want us to be. We make mistakes and become more exhausted from overthinking, and we become angry. We explode with righteous indignation. "Don't they know who we are?" "Don't they know how hard we have worked?" But in reality we chose to hide our true identity. We did not respect our own or other people's free will. We create a mental prison that is made up from shaming beliefs about ourselves. We don't care about boundaries – we are focused on holding others hostage. We become enmeshed in others and lose our identities.

In the absence of a caregiver attuned to our needs, we, the abused and neglected children, soon learn to take care of our own needs. We are the children who are often admired for our maturity beyond our years and are a relief to our caregivers, teachers, and later our bosses.

We are the lonely "self starters" who are a "pleasure to work with" because we require little or no supervision; we are the quiet neighbor who rarely talks to anyone, and the compliant partner in relationships. The "payoff" for us is that we ward off any disappointment by not allowing ourselves to express any needs to anyone or to admit that we need anything. The denial of our needs is a small price to pay to avoid the overwhelming sense of loss buried under layers of self-sufficiency. (**The Other Laundry List**)

In the process of recovery, we learn to identify ourselves and our needs each time we say, "My name is Henry and I am an adult child." By this simple act we begin to take responsibility for ourselves and not depend on anyone to tell us who we are or how we "should" act. In fact, attending ACA meetings and associating with other adult children is an expression of a need of our True Self, and the ACA fellowship meets that need by accepting us just the way we are without any preconditions. (**The Flip Side of The Laundry List**)

As time passes, we may begin to free our True Self from the intricate web of denial that we created to sustain us in the alcoholic or dysfunctional families we were raised in. By regularly attending and participating in fellowship meetings, taking the ACA Twelve Steps, and reparenting ourselves, we are beginning the process of moving out of the sanctuary we had built for our True Self and become part of the fellowship that celebrates our individuality. No longer alone, we can take the ACA Steps to become the person we were meant to be or want to be instead of the person who we became to satisfy the needs of our caregivers. (**The Flip Side of The Other Laundry List**)

ORIENTATION
Be Prepared to Engage Your Senses

Look at some things (actual)
Make a noise
Eat a peach
Smell some cinnamon
Pat your face

Trait 2 Reflections

The Laundry List

We became approval seekers and lost our identity in the process.

1. As a child, what prompted me to seek approval?

2. In what ways do I behave more as an approval-seeker; how do I lose my identity in the process?

3. How did losing my identity help me in my childhood? When and why do I continue to not claim my true identity in my adulthood?

4. What identity or identities did I focus on as a child? How did that focus help me survive?

5. If I weren't raised in a dysfunctional/alcoholic home, what type of identity might I have had?

6. Describe how your true identity (being valued for who you truly are) has been hidden/ suppressed (for example, by being your caretakers and/or loved ones wanted you to be). How did this happen in your childhood? How has it been hidden in your adult life?

7. When you answer questions like this, do you anticipate "what they want to hear" and hope to get it "right"? Have you taken tests or completed forms and filled in the blanks as you "knew" they wanted to hear? Have you answered the questions to "get what you wanted" after the form would be read, perhaps for some service?

The Other Laundry List
To avoid becoming enmeshed and entangled with other people and losing ourselves in the process, we become rigidly self-sufficient. We disdain the approval of others.

1. Describe ways you see enmeshment or unhealthy boundaries in your relationships.

2. Describe ways you see healthy boundaries in your relationships.

3. Describe ways you might be rigidly self-sufficient.

4. Do I find myself disdaining approval of others? How do I externally and internally act out my disdain of others? Provide some examples.

5. What did I learn to do when I was little to take care of myself because no one was taking care of me in this way?

6. What happened when I was entangled and/or enmeshed with others as a child?

7. What happens internally when someone tries to get close to me when I'm not ready?

The Flip Side of The Laundry List
We do not depend on others to tell us who we are.

1. Describe ways you do not depend on others to define who you are.

2. How could you integrate more ways *not* to depend on others to tell you who you are?

3. Who am I and how do I know this?

4. What happens internally when someone describes me and speaks for me or states my opinion when I am standing right there?

5. Describe someone's perspective of you to the best of your ability and then describe how that perspective makes you feel.

6. When someone draws an inaccurate assumption involving you, what do you do and/or say?

The Flip Side of The Other Laundry List

We realize the sanctuary we have built to protect the frightened and injured child within has become a prison and we become willing to risk moving out of isolation.

1. When you are alone, do you feel more like it is a prison – or a sanctuary?

2. Describe ways you have been or are willing to risk moving out of isolation.

3. Describe your past concept of a sanctuary type of isolation and the benefits you seemed to receive from building it and living in it.

4. What are some instances and experiences that helped you realize that your sanctuary has become a prison?

5. What were some of my first steps in moving out of isolation?

6. What are some of the benefits of moving out of isolation?

TRAIT
THREE

Trait 3

The Laundry List	The Other Laundry List
We are frightened by angry people and any personal criticism.	*We frighten people with our anger and threat of belittling criticism.*
The Flip Side of The Laundry List	**The Flip Side of The Other Laundry List**
We are not automatically frightened by angry people and no longer regard personal criticism as a threat.	*With our renewed sense of self-worth and self-esteem we realize it is no longer necessary to protect ourselves by intimidating others with contempt, ridicule and anger.*

*A*lcoholism and addiction are very angry and destructive solutions to a spiritual dilemma. The families we grew up with were usually loaded with hostility, both spoken and unspoken. As a result of our early exposure to this anger and the accompanying criticism, we became sensitive to any actual or potential expression of anger or criticism. In an oftentimes angry world, we may have become avid anger and criticism avoiders. In the Game of Dissociation, this is the victim position that gave us some solace, but also made us prone to being victimized even more. Out of sheer necessity, we "dosed" ourselves with the inside drugs of worry (cortisol), fear (adrenaline), and pain (melatonin) to numb ourselves of our feelings, because the trauma and loss we experienced were too great for our tiny bodies to withstand. (**The Laundry List**)

Instead of being anger and criticism avoiders, some of us became angry and critical, thinking "If we can't beat them, we'll join them!" We anger easily or offer cutting "helpful" criticism, especially if the object of our anger or criticism reminds us of our own buried vulnerabilities. We think a hard dose of "tough love" is a jolt of reality that is in others' best interest. Such "truth" without compassion is hurtful and reflects our desensitization or dissociation from our own vulnerable True Self. Unchecked, we will gather around us only those who can withstand the constant barrage of anger and criticism that we carry inside ourselves. We "dose" ourselves with the adrenaline we get from taking charge and controlling others. This tactic of the Game of Dissociation blocks our painful memories and feelings of the hurt we experienced as children. (**The Other Laundry List**)

At ACA meetings we begin the process of learning to trust again. First we trust that the meeting will be there and that we can share without being judged or criticized. Then we begin to trust the members to be available as fellow travelers. These meetings provide a space for us to learn to view angry people as folks who are expressing pain, fear, grief, or sadness, and that it doesn't necessarily have anything to do with us. At some point we may realize that another's anger or criticism did not threaten us or make us run away. The miracle of recovery has begun to take hold. (**The Flip Side of The Laundry List**)

If we are working the suggested program of recovery we will soon realize that we no longer need to express contempt, ridicule or anger to defend our false self and that we are comfortable with who we are. Our renewed True Self esteem and True Self worth allows us to admit we are humans and very likely to make mistakes. If someone is angry with us, we can hear them out, ask ourselves what, if anything, we might have done to harm the person. If nothing is of our doing we simply say, "Thank you for sharing. I am sorry you feel that way."

No longer petrified with the fear of anger, we can stand in the present and take responsibility for our mistakes when we find we are in the wrong. Even criticism may be viewed from this emotionally sober perspective. We can hear the observations of others, sit with it and see if there is some truth to what is being shared that could be to our benefit. If there is, we can thank the person for showing us an aspect of ourselves that otherwise we probably wouldn't have seen. If it doesn't resonate as true to us, we can set it aside until it might be relevant. "If it doesn't apply, let it fly." (**The Flip Side of The Other Laundry List**)

ORIENTATION
Be Prepared to Engage Your Senses

Look at some things (actual)
Make a noise
Eat a peach
Smell some cinnamon
Pat your face

Trait 3 Reflections

The Laundry List

We are frightened by angry people and any personal criticism.

1. Describe ways you are frightened by angry people (both in childhood memories as well as in your adult relationships).

2. Describe ways you are frightened by personal criticism (both in childhood memories as well as in your adult relationships).

3. Can you see ways you've dissociated – "dosed" yourself with inside drugs to numb yourself – to avoid feeling fear?

4. Make a list of the people who were angry and critical in your childhood.

5. Make a list of the comments that you heard and the physical acts that caused you to fear angry people and any personal criticism.

6. Who in your present life comes to mind as being similar physically, vocally, or in demeanor to the angry and critical people in your childhood?

7. Who are the types of people and the types of criticism that are the most powerful in causing your fear today as an adult?

The Other Laundry List

We frighten people with our anger and threat of belittling criticism.

1. Describe ways you frighten people with your anger.

2. Describe ways you frighten people with belittling criticism, or cutting "helpful" criticism.

3. Who have you frightened with your anger and your threat of belittling criticism?

4. What are some examples of actions you have taken to frighten people in this way?

5. How have you threatened people physically, verbally, and/or emotionally?

6. Can you see ways you "dose" yourself with the adrenaline you get from taking charge and controlling others, and how this blocks your painful memories and feelings of the hurt you experienced in childhood? List some examples.

The Flip Side of The Laundry List

We are not automatically frightened by angry people and no longer regard personal criticism as a threat.

1. Describe ways you've grown not to be automatically frightened by angry people.

2. Describe ways you've grown not to be automatically regard personal criticism as a threat.

3. Can you identify times you are feeling your feelings around this trait rather than "dosing" yourself to numb and avoid these fears?

4. List the ACA Steps and/or ACA Traditions and/or other program tools you have found that help support a true perspective of personal criticism and angry people.

5. Describe an example of an improved relationship you've experienced due to not being afraid of that person.

6. Describe a group or a type of person with whom your comfort level has improved, where in times past you would have been uncomfortable.

7. Describe an experience when you were personally criticized and you could tell that you had changed due to your ACA recovery.

8. Which ACA Promise or Promises do you see that are coming true as you see your progress in relation to this?

The Flip Side of The Other Laundry List

With our renewed sense of self-worth and self-esteem we realize it is no longer necessary to protect ourselves by intimidating others with contempt, ridicule and anger.

1. Describe times when you've realized it is no longer necessary to protect yourself by intimidating others with contempt, ridicule, and anger.

2. Describe times when your renewed True Self esteem and worth have empowered you to admit you are human and make mistakes. How did that feel?

3. Describe times when you have been able to soberly hear the observations of others, reflect on these observations, and see if there is some truth to what is being shared that could be to your benefit.

4. Describe in detail your self-worth before ACA and your self-worth now.

5. Which ACA tools do you attribute to this growth and progress that you've observed in your life?

6. When you feel angry today, what do you do?

TRAIT
FOUR

Trait 4

The Laundry List	The Other Laundry List
We either become alcoholics, marry them, or both, or find another compulsive personality such as a workaholic to fulfill our sick abandonment needs.	*We dominate others and abandon them before they can abandon us or we avoid relationships with dependent people altogether. To avoid being hurt, we isolate and dissociate and thereby abandon ourselves.*
The Flip Side of The Laundry List	**The Flip Side of The Other Laundry List**
We do not have a compulsive need to recreate abandonment.	*We accept and comfort the isolated and hurt inner child we have abandoned and disavowed and thereby end the need to act out our fears of enmeshment and abandonment with other people.*

*T*hose of us fortunate to have recovery from alcohol or substances other than alcohol (so called "dry goods") refer to ourselves as double winners. Having been an addict or alcoholic, and having begun the process of recovery from addiction by the time we reached ACA, we found we had more work to do. Perhaps we ended up with a mate who was an alcoholic or substance abuser, or perhaps had another compulsive personality or was a rage-aholic. In a real sense we had chosen to be with partners who would help us play out the abandonment we experienced as children. As difficult as it may seem, when we are honest and look at our relationships carefully, we can see that either we chose to be with people who were otherwise unavailable or that, over time, we provoked their abandonment. In the Game of Dissociation, we assumed the role of rescuer. In time, we either became a victim or victimizer. (**The Laundry List**)

For some of us the idea of becoming an alcoholic was turned upside down. Instead of becoming dependent on alcohol or some other outside substance, we chose to dose ourselves with an internal concoction of pain, fear and excitement. By becoming the dominant player, we controlled the ebb and flow of our relationships. With this tactic, we chose to connect only with those we could keep at arm's length. We created a conflicted dynamic of being in a relationship with another person – without intimacy. When the relationship seemed to veer toward intimacy, we withdrew, isolated and dissociated. The end result was no different than with the alcoholic or dysfunctional family – we protected our True Self by creating a false self to hide our authentic needs and wants. (**The Other Laundry List**)

The Game of Dissociation allows us to be either the abandoned (victim) of **The Laundry List**, or and abandoner (victimizer) of **The Other Laundry List** – in an endlessly repetitive cycle to not remember or remind ourselves of our traumatic childhood experiences.

Our ACA work gives us many gifts. Steady, daily Step work with a fellow traveler, regular attendance at meetings, and giving service from a place of love helps us realize that our habit to form unhealthy relationships reveals the conflict between our desire for closeness and our fear of intimacy. The layers of denial are carefully revealed and gently pulled away. It is important to remember that reparenting involves more than getting in touch with feelings and buried memories. We also can take an emotional inventory of our patterns of bonding that may reveal how we recreate or recycle our abandonment. (**The Flip Side of The Laundry List**)

The process of reparenting starts before we attend our first ACA meeting. The bottoms we hit prepare us to receive the gift of recovery and, after a while, we realize we couldn't have been willing unless we had hit our bottom. We can finally allow ourselves to reach out and ask for help.

In ACA we are shown that we can make the space for our inner loving parent to step in and begin building a relationship with our wounded and lonely Inner Child. As with any relationship, this process takes time and effort. This is a commitment we have to keep to nurture a trusting relationship. The more we connect our Inner Child with our inner loving parent, the more the fears of being engulfed or annihilated are reduced and eventually eliminated. As we enter a relationship we bring these new gifts with us and create true and lasting intimacy primarily with our True Self and subsequently with those who are equally available to us to bond with. (**The Flip Side of The Other Laundry List**)

ORIENTATION
Be Prepared to Engage Your Senses

Look at some things (actual)
Make a noise
Eat a peach
Smell some cinnamon
Pat your face

Trait 4 Reflections

The Laundry List

We either become alcoholics, marry them or both, or find another compulsive personality such as a workaholic to fulfill our sick abandonment needs.

1. Who in your adult life is the closest personality type to the most significant adult in your childhood who influenced you?

2. List the various compulsions of significant others from your childhood.

3. List the various compulsions of significant others from your adulthood.

4. List the various compulsions of yourself, both past and present.

5. How does being involved with another compulsive personality fulfill your abandonment "needs"?

6. Describe an instance when a compulsive personality was no longer in your life and how it affected you.

The Other Laundry List

We dominate others and abandon them before they can abandon us or we avoid relationships with dependent people altogether. To avoid being hurt, we isolate and dissociate and thereby abandon ourselves.

1. List the people/jobs/events/groups you've abandoned in your life and how you felt each time you made the decision to leave and what contributed to your leaving.

2. How do you dissociate?

3. In what ways do you feel others can hurt you?

4. Do you study people in order to see if they are "safe"? If you do this, list examples of what constitutes a "safe" person.

5. Who have you dominated in the past, and who dominated you in childhood and adulthood?

The Flip Side of The Laundry List
We do not have a compulsive need to recreate abandonment.

1. Which ACA Steps or ACA Traditions have helped you lessen your compulsive need to recreate abandonment and/or helped you identify this compulsive need learned in childhood?

2. Describe a time in your life when you did recreate abandonment and a time in your present life when you could tell that you weren't recreating abandonment and you were true to yourself.

3. Using your imagination, describe yourself from an outsider's point of view as to how you may have appeared in the past when you were acting out your compulsion or compulsions.

4. Describe a scenario that would detail the progress you are making in not having a compulsive need to recreate abandonment.

The Flip Side of The Other Laundry List

We accept and comfort the isolated and hurt Inner Child we have abandoned and disavowed and thereby end the need to act out our fears of enmeshment and abandonment with other people.

1. Describe as if you were telling a fellow traveler: what you do when you comfort your isolated and hurt Inner Child, and give a recent example of when you've done that.

2. How do you communicate the acceptance you feel for your Inner Child in all of the aspects, moods, needs, and wants that your Inner Child displays?

3. How have you been disavowed by others in your past and in your adulthood?

4. How have you disavowed yourself in your past and in your adulthood?

5. Are there any similarities or patterns that you see that have encouraged you to remain alone?

6. When someone enters your life and it appears that you are moving into a closer stage of your relationship, how different do you feel now than before you were in ACA?

TRAIT
FIVE

Trait 5

The Laundry List	The Other Laundry List
We live life from the viewpoint of victims and we are attracted by that weakness in our love and friendship relationships.	*We live life from the standpoint of a victimizer, and are attracted to people we can manipulate and control in our important relationships.*
The Flip Side of The Laundry List	**The Flip Side of The Other Laundry List**
We stop living life from the standpoint of victims and are not attracted by this trait in our important relationships.	*Because we are whole and complete we no longer try to control others through manipulation and force and bind them to us with fear in order to avoid feeling isolated and alone.*

*A*s children, we were subjected to a constant assault of our sensibilities. Whether our parents drank or not, our dysfunctional families bound us in their toxic mix of hurt and anguish coupled with denial and defiance. There is no admission fee to the Game of Dissociation. All members of the family are, unfortunately, given one of four roles in the game: victim, victimizer, rescuer I, or rescuer II. As a result of this conditioning, we grew up feeling disempowered and unable to make healthy choices. Disconnected from our own feelings and our sense of power, we go through our lives being blown about by the winds of the times, neither realizing our abilities nor recognizing that we chose relationships with people who will prey on our inability to exercise our power. Usually with a shrug of resignation, we accepted our situation as our fate – unable to break free from the compulsion to recreate and recycle this unhealthy dissociative habit. (**The Laundry List**)

Somehow during all the chaos visited upon us in our childhoods, we were taught that the weaker members were losers and we became determined to be among the winners. This meant that we became the victimizer or rescuer II. Either passively or actively, we exercised our power beyond the requirements of the situations. In fact, we chose to bring into our circle only those who we could manipulate to be subservient. These submissive members reinforce our "strength" and we feed the refortification of our take charge defenses. If someone challenged our power, we somehow distanced ourselves from them or provoked their sudden departure. The specter of losing our victimizer role was too threatening to us. (**The Other Laundry List**)

The process of emotional recovery is not a solitary event. Going to meetings, sharing honestly, chatting after the meeting either in person or over the phone – all of these gives us an opportunity to exercise greater power in incremental but progressive ways. Instead of feeling helpless, we are encouraged by what we see, hear, and read in our ACA meetings. The veil of denial, which seemed like a thick, immovable tapestry, now seems like a sheer satin sheet easily moved by us when we are ready. Now, as we approach our day, we see the opportunities to stop viewing life from the perspective of what is happening to us, and become able to see ourselves as a participant in those instances. We exercise discernment when choosing to be in a relationship, observing the person with whom we are trying to connect with for their ability to be responsible for themselves and not looking for us to be the decision maker. (**The Flip Side of The Laundry List**)

Throughout the course of our ACA Step work and reparenting, we have been learning about and applying the concepts of critical survival inner parent, inner loving parent, Inner Child, and our Higher Power. We have achieved a sense of wholeness and completeness because of this painstaking work and can see that controlling others is a form of acting out the same behaviors that beset our families. When tempted or lured into a situation where control and manipulation seem to be the answer, we change the question. Instead of "How can I dominate?" we might ask, "How can I humbly participate?" If someone is starting to walk away from us, we no longer resist their leaving, and instead use the ACA Twelve Steps and reparenting to comfort our Inner Child. No longer fearful of being alone or isolated, we recognize the opportunity to deepen our ACA Step work with our inner loving parent, our Inner Child, our Higher Power, and our critical survival inner parent. (**The Flip Side of The Other Laundry List**)

ORIENTATION
Be Prepared to Engage Your Senses

Look at some things (actual)
Make a noise
Eat a peach
Smell some cinnamon
Pat your face

Trait 5 Reflections

The Laundry List

We live life from the viewpoint of victims and we are attracted by that weakness in our love and friendship relationships.

1. Describe the characteristics of anyone you've known in the past who lived life from the viewpoint of a victim.

2. Describe the characteristics of anyone you know in the present who lives life from the viewpoint of a victim.

3. Given the opportunity to talk to someone who looks sad and down at a party and is sitting alone, or the chance to talk to a smiling effervescent person in a circle of other happy looking people, where would you feel the most comfortable? Why is this so?

4. List some phrases that might come out of a person's mouth who is living life from the viewpoint of a victim. What are some of the thoughts that might swirl around in their head?

5. Describe a relationship that you were involved in as a child where you were a victim.

6. Describe a relationship from your adulthood where you were the victim.

The Other Laundry List

We live life from the standpoint of a victimizer, and are attracted to people we can manipulate and control in our important relationships.

1. If you had to describe your idea of the "textbook" victimizer, what attributes would that person have?

2. Have you had the ability to see victimizing traits in others easily while it is more difficult to attribute victimizing traits to yourself?

3. Do you "keep your thoughts to yourself" because these thoughts are often extreme in nature; such as belittling, judging, ridiculing, and/or "rolling your eyes" at others?

4. Have others said to you that they don't feel that you are a safe person, or that they limit the time they spend with you, or they wish you could be a little "nicer"? What behaviors could you be exhibiting to precipitate these comments?

5. Who have you manipulated in your past? Do you find yourself intrigued by people who are under-educated, physically impaired, mentally struggling, or not able to speak fluently? Are you drawn to someone who is lost and in need of directions? Do you rush to help someone who is walking to a door with their hands full? Do you have a strong urge to guide, lead, and watch out for the comfort of ACA newcomers to "make sure" they come back and feel a part of the group?

6. Do you get a powerful surge or reaction inside when you are recognized for "helping" someone more disadvantaged than yourself? Is this surge so powerful that you look for more opportunities to "help" others?

The Flip Side of The Laundry List

We stop living life from the standpoint of victims and are not attracted by this trait in our important relationships.

1. Describe what a relationship would look like where two people are equals. Who do you relate to in this way?

2. When things "go wrong" in everyday life now, how are your thoughts and your responses different than before you found ACA?

3. What "self-talk" do you practice as a daily habit, or in times of stress? What ACA affirmations have helped you?

4. Before you were in ACA, when you were with a fairly confident and healthy person who could pause and speak out, sharing a different viewpoint from your own, how did it feel? How does it feel now?

5. Would you describe yourself as a fairly confident and healthy person who can pause and speak your mind, and share a different viewpoint from the person with whom you're conversing? If this is true, to what do you attribute these changes in you?

The Flip Side of The Other Laundry List

Because we are whole and complete we no longer try to control others through manipulation and force and bind them to us with fear in order to avoid feeling isolated and alone.

1. Which ACA tools do you attribute to the growth and progress that you've observed in your life in relation to the **Flip Side of The Other Laundry List** of Trait 5?

2. Describe what felt empty and incomplete in you before you found ACA and started progressing in your ACA process of recovery. Describe what feels whole and complete in you now.

3. Which ACA Promise or Promises do you see that are coming true as you view your progress in relation to becoming whole and complete?

4. When you were alone in your childhood, how did that feel?

5. When you were alone in your adulthood (before ACA), how did that feel?

6. How does it feel now when you are alone?

7. When you are alone, are you in the quiet or do you have many activities happening?

8. Are you able to be alone, in silence, with nothing happening?

TRAIT
SIX

Trait 6

The Laundry List	The Other Laundry List
We have an overdeveloped sense of responsibility and it is easier* for us to be concerned with others rather than ourselves. This enables us not to look too closely at our own faults.	*We are irresponsible and self-centered. Our inflated sense of self-worth and self-importance prevents us from seeing our deficiencies and shortcomings.*
The Flip Side of The Laundry List	**The Flip Side of The Other Laundry List**
We do not use enabling as a way to avoid looking at our own shortcomings.	*Through our in-depth inventory we discover our true identity as capable, worthwhile people. By asking to have our shortcomings removed we are freed from the burden of inferiority and grandiosity.*

*A*s babies and young children we have a natural belief that we are omnipotent. The baby who cries and then sees her caregiver appear believes that her crying magically produces her caregiver. As young children our sense of having magical powers is overused to give us a sense of normalcy in the chaotic and destructive families we were raised in. We assumed that since we had magical powers, we could control the caregivers and families that were acting crazily. We would be responsible even though their behavior was not our responsibility and was beyond our control.

This rescuer role in the Game of Dissociation allows us momentary pause before defaulting into either a victim or victimizer role. The internal dosing goes from adrenaline (excitement) to cortisol (worry) to an internal speedball. As adults, this tactic became a habit where we always assumed over-responsibility for others because it gave us an excuse not to look at ourselves. The discomfort of honestly looking at ourselves, our pain, and our losses was easily overshadowed by our inclination – our habit – of looking for others for whom we could be "responsible". Meanwhile the unexpressed feelings and memories from our traumatic childhood continue festering, to be acted out repeatedly, producing a paradoxical mixture of us being "helpful" to others, while injurious to our True Self. (**The Laundry List**)

---

* It is probably more accurate to say hypervigilance made it *necessary* for us as children to focus on others so that we could survive. Preferring and choosing come from higher order thinking and reasoning capacities that most adult children do not yet have conscious, consistent access to. It is not that we disregard our own faults out of some sort of conscious preference as adults – as children we were completely busy looking outward to survive. As adults, when we *do* examine our own faults, we are almost always looking destructively, in a self-critical manner. We continue this pattern until we learn otherwise – after a great deal of focused therapy and recovery. With the majority of ACAs coming from this state of hypervigilance and self criticism, we simply don't yet know how to look at ourselves in a constructive way.

The sheer weight of all that responsibility becomes too much to bear by a solitary human being, and the tendency is to go in the opposite direction: Instead of being overly responsible, we dissociate from our responsibilities. We become so engrossed in our false self that what is important to others doesn't matter to us. Instead of being appropriately responsible, we strategize that if people just took care of themselves everybody would be okay. This increased level of false self attention worsens over time and alienates those around us. Armed with this false self-importance, we act out on our loved ones, co-workers, and friends the very deficiencies and shortcomings that we suffered from in our childhoods. Our false self-centeredness keeps us blinded to our deficiencies or shortcomings when we stand so close to our defensive false self. (**The Other Laundry List**)

The ACA inventory through the Twelve Steps and Twelve Traditions is in-depth and painstaking, but has as its reward a relief from the burden of taking care of everyone and the realization of our True Self. No longer bound by our "magical powers," we can enjoy being a fellow ACA with our ACA family, our loved ones, coworkers, and friends. Our True Self shines through and we can admit, accept, and be the capable and worthwhile individuals that we were intended to be. Allowing others to bear the brunt of their own decisions and not attempting to control their actions restores a great deal of our energy and power. (**The Flip Side of The Laundry List**)

As we continue to use the ACA Steps and Traditions to better understand and integrate our traits, we are clear where our behavior is enabling and, with our Higher Power's grace, able to abstain without any sense of grandiosity or judgmentalness in the full knowledge that only one's Higher Power has the ability to grant someone the courage to change themselves. Left to face our inner hurts and memories, the torrent of unexpressed emotions eventually subsides and allows us to be emotionally, psychologically, physically, and spiritually present foremost for our Inner Child and then for others. If we dedicate ourselves to this life restoring process, our spirit's majesty awakens. (**The Flip Side of The Other Laundry List**)

ORIENTATION
Be Prepared to Engage Your Senses

Look at some things (actual)
Make a noise
Eat a peach
Smell some cinnamon
Pat your face

Trait 6 Reflections

The Laundry List

We have an overdeveloped sense of responsibility and it is easier for us to be concerned with others rather than ourselves. This enables us not to look too closely at our own faults.

1. List in detail the responsibilities you had as a child that you now know were too much responsibility for you at your age. Next, describe how each of those responsibilities made you feel.

2. List in detail who you were concerned about (focused on) as a child and how this concern and focus affected you. How did it affect your feelings or your ability to be a child?

3. Why did you focus on these people? What would have happened if you only focused on yourself and your needs as a child?

4. Make a detailed list of the likes and dislikes of three highly significant people in your life who you have focused on. Describe in detail what this exercise brought up for you.

5. List your parent(s) or caregiver(s) faults and shortcomings. List your own faults today as an adult. Which list was easier to make?

6. Is it possible that your faults and shortcomings make sense and are acceptable because of the way you were raised, while your caregiver's faults and shortcomings don't make sense and are not acceptable because of the way they were raised?

7. Did you feel hesitant in listing your own faults? What prompted the hesitance? What happened as a child when your faults were shown, addressed, or pointed out?

8. There are many phrases in the ACA Twelve Steps that some members have difficulty with. These difficulties stem from looking at themselves and from past childhood shaming. Write in detail what comes to mind *immediately* when you read each phrase below, and why you think that is your initial reaction:

   • Defects of character:

   • Exact nature of our wrongs:

   • When we were wrong promptly admitted it:

• Willing to make amends to them all:

• Made a list of all persons we had harmed:

• Could restore us to sanity:

• Our lives had become unmanageable:

The Other Laundry List

We are irresponsible and self-centered. Our inflated sense of self-worth and self-importance prevents us from seeing our deficiencies and shortcomings.

1. List the self-centered and irresponsible people who you encountered while growing up.

2. Describe in a separate list what you think made these people self-centered and irresponsible. Circle items in this list that are similar to the dysfunctions that you learned and that became a part of your false self.

3. Make a list of people in your childhood who were not irresponsible.

4. Make a list of people in your childhood who were not self-centered.

5. It has been said that "when you are pointing out another person's deficiencies it is because you have the same deficiencies". Do you think this is true? Have you ever experienced being irritated by someone who is similar to you? Were you able to see similarities between yourself and the person who you found irritating? Did you instead think that they were the "cause" of your frustration, and if they would change, you would feel better and the situation would resolve? Write examples of these situations.

6. How do you feel when someone tells you that you have made a mistake which resulted in a problem? Do you have a tendency to shift blame or minimize the results? Do you wish that no one had seen the mistake that was made? After such a conversation, do you review what was said and wish you had said something different? Do you review the conversation again, adding more to what you had said before? Do you find your mind keeps returning to this dialog?

The Flip Side of The Laundry List

We do not use enabling as a way to avoid looking at our own shortcomings.

1. Describe the characteristics of a person who you would consider an enabler. What do you think are some motivations for this person you've described?

2. Who have you observed in your life that played out the role of enabler? When have you played that role? What was your motivation?

3. What types of people or situations seem to bring out the enabler in you? Are there types of people who usually *do not* bring out the enabler in you? If so, why do you think that is?

4. As far as your physical energy is concerned, does paying attention to others seem to use up a great deal of your personal energy? If and when you focus on yourself instead of others, do you find that you have more energy for yourself? What ACA tools have helped you see yourself more clearly?

5. What parts of the ACA program do you think are helping you progress from enabler to living a life that is more self-focused and self-caring? When you first started living in a self-focused way, describe how it felt then, and how it feels now.

6. By *not* using enabling as a way to avoid looking at your own shortcomings, which ACA Promises are coming true for you?

The Flip Side of The Other Laundry List

Through our in-depth inventory we discover our true identity as capable, worthwhile people. By asking to have our shortcomings removed we are freed from the burden of inferiority and grandiosity.

1. As a child, if you were raised in a caring, supportive home the words "capable" and "worthwhile" probably would have been used in affirming you. What other words would caring and supportive parents have used to describe and affirm you? What does your Loving Parent and Higher Power say to you about you? Are you more able to give those words to yourself now that you have found ACA?

2. As best as you can, list the words that describe who you were inside as a young child.

3. List the words that describe your True Self/Inner Child as you know it to be now.

4. Which worksheets and exercises in your ACA literature have helped you to find your true identity? List in detail how your Higher Power and/or Loving Parent and/or Inner Child would describe you.

5. Which ACA Promises are coming true for you through your in-depth inventory?

6. List three primary reasons for your progress.

7. Describe situations in which you would have reacted with inferiority before you found ACA. Describe situations in which you would have reacted with grandiosity before you found ACA. Using those same situations, describe how you would respond now. Compare the similarities and the differences.

8. List how you believe you impact your ACA group and your ACA friends and any service that you are performing. Though no one expects perfection, would you say that you are acting more from your false self or your True Self today?

9. Imagine what it would be like to live with yourself if the pre-ACA version of you were your roommate. Write in detail what that might be like.

TRAIT
SEVEN

Trait 7

The Laundry List	The Other Laundry List
We get guilt feelings when we stand up for ourselves instead of giving in to others.	*We make others feel guilty when they attempt to assert themselves.*
The Flip Side of The Laundry List	**The Flip Side of The Other Laundry List**
We do not feel guilty when we stand up for ourselves.	*We support and encourage others in their efforts to be assertive.*

*P*erhaps the greatest loss we suffered as children in an alcoholic or dysfunctional family was losing our ability to stand up for ourselves. The aggressive demand by the family to deny what was actually happening was extraordinary and, for a defenseless child, overwhelming. As children, instead of challenging the family's denial system, we played the only role we could, which was to passively give in (submit) to the family's denial system to survive the impact of the alcoholic or dysfunctional family. By giving in, we are unconsciously playing our role in the Game of Dissociation and receiving a payoff of not feeling our feelings.

Although we may have sensed that our submission was wrong, we denied our truth by self-betrayal and self-abandonment, or betrayed and abandoned ourself, or died countless small deaths as we joined in the dysfunction of denying the obvious and, in turn, denied our True Self the birthright of expression. This interaction was repeated regularly, even hourly, until it became routine for us to deny ourself and give in to the conscious or unconscious demands of the family system. So deeply ingrained was this habit that we can read another's body posture, tone of voice, or facial expressions. Even before our own perception can be formulated we act out our passive/submissive role, thwarting any awareness of having our own viewpoint. We preempt any thought of our own beliefs or needs by our constant scanning of those we interact with for their needs, and react to fill those needs, cost us what it may. Thus robbed of our inner senses, we wander and wonder, "Where am I in all this?" (**The Laundry List**)

Having been conditioned by the family dysfunction to submit and deny, or bury, or perish our True Self, some of us chose to survive by becoming the aggressors or perpetrators. While we still survey our surroundings to get a lay of the land, we especially watch for and target those whose views would hold greater sway than us and we attack them. Sometimes our attacks are indirect slights; other attacks may be more of a full frontal assault. Whether we chose a passive or aggressive form of acting out, our overriding goal is to prevent the other person from asserting any kind of expression of their True Self. Our ulterior motive is to hide our own hurts and feelings developed from having been similarly denounced as children. In this dissociative game, we take away the other person's ability to share their view so we can keep our own view of our own deprivations locked away in our subconscious. The payoff is a false sense of mastery, domination, and control. This usually leads other people to either turn away from us or be drawn to the dysfunctional form of control we exhibit. Either way, we lose our ability to be genuine, human, and to express our buried hurts and feelings. (**The Other Laundry List**)

As we embark on this spiritual voyage to wholeness, one of the first ports of call is our ability to feel and express ourselves at ACA meetings. Here no one interrupts us, makes comments about our shares, or judges us, because what we say is true for us. This safe environment gives us the opportunity to delve deeper into the unconsciously assumed roles we adopted as children. Usually in a gradual manner, our sacrifices are grieved with the other ACA members witnessing us with empathy. As we continue on this spiritual quest, we may find that sharing our truth produces choppy waters, an occasional swell, or some other unfavorable condition. Here, the inner compass we have reconnected to, along with the ACA Steps and ACA Traditions, gives us the confidence we need to stay on course. Even when we may have strayed from our course, the ACA Steps allow us to re-adjust our bearings and correct our direction until we reach our goal, or reach the road of happy destiny where we will be free to explore the world as the happy, joyous, and free individuals we were meant to be. (**The Flip Side of The Laundry List**)

In ACA the most hurt people on the planet are welcomed with open arms, hearts, and ears. Once we have found ACA, it is suggested that we find a fellow traveler to journey with. In these spiritual teams, we venture backward and forward with action coming from love, understanding, and patience. At first, this unconditional support may threaten our sensibility. After all, we have never had support and encouragement at this level, but over time we can re-build the trust that allows us to explore the furthest recesses of our subconscious minds to explore the roots of traumatizing childhoods. We emerge emotionally sober and confident of our views and are supported and encouraged by our groups, our fellow travelers, our inner loving parent, our Inner Child(ren), and our inner Higher Power. This outer team and the inner crew help us find our True Self, learn to discern when it is time to be assertive, and quietly cheer us on to deeper levels of trust and empowerment. What may have started out as a raft became a boat and is now a ship of love and goodwill for all who may venture into our meetings and have the gift of willingness.

ORIENTATION
Be Prepared to Engage Your Senses

Look at some things (actual)
Make a noise
Eat a peach
Smell some cinnamon
Pat your face

Trait 7 Reflections

The Laundry List
We get guilt feelings when we stand up for ourselves instead of giving in to others.

1. If someone were inside your head when you had thoughts of guilt for standing up for yourself, what thoughts would they hear running through your mind?

2. In what situations is it hard for you to stand up for yourself? When is it easier for you to stand up for yourself?

3. What is the "payoff" for giving in to others?

4. When you "give in" to another person, how do you feel about that person afterward?

5. Have you "given in" to a person when they didn't ask you to give in? If so, what motivated you to "give in"?

6. As a child, did you ever stand up for yourself? If so, describe what happened.

7. As a child, did you see another person get "in trouble" for standing up for themselves, or standing up for you? If so, describe the situation(s).

The Other Laundry List

We make others feel guilty when they attempt to assert themselves.

1. What techniques have you used to make someone feel guilty for attempting to assert themselves?

2. What techniques were used on you as a child to make you feel guilty for standing up for yourself?

3. What techniques did you observe being used on others when they stood up for themselves?

4. What guilt-inducing actions do you remember observing in your childhood? List guilt-inducing actions you observed in caregivers, siblings, relatives, teachers, authority figures, religious figures, etc.

5. What messages did you hear as a child about people who assert themselves?

6. When someone asserts themselves, do you experience an internal discomfort? If so, describe what your thoughts are in that moment. Is there a link from your childhood to your adulthood in this discomfort?

The Flip Side of The Laundry List

We do not feel guilty when we stand up for ourselves.

1. Have you had a situation lately where you stood up for yourself and you felt pretty calm about it? If so, describe the situation in detail.

2. Describe in detail any progress that you have seen in asserting yourself since finding ACA.

3. Make two lists for standing up for yourself: Easier Situations and Harder Situations. Describe in detail why you think some are easier and some are harder.

4. As a child, did you ever stand up for yourself with a "safe" person? What was that like?

5. Describe a person who you've seen standing up for themselves in a healthy way. What does it look like? How do you feel when you observe this happening? What do you think when you see someone standing up for themselves?

The Flip Side of The Other Laundry List

We support and encourage others in their efforts to be assertive.

1. In your ACA group, how do you feel when you observe an adult child changing over time in their ability to be assertive? What progress have you seen in this person?

2. How would you describe your progress in supporting and encouraging others in their efforts to be assertive? Describe your progress in relationships, jobs, ACA recovery, etc.

3. Has a fellow traveler reached out to you to get your perspective on their situation, or asked for your experience in a similar situation? Did this result in your fellow traveler's feeling encouraged and supported? If so, describe how this interaction affected you physically, mentally, emotionally, and spiritually.

4. Which ACA Promise(s) are coming true for you as you progress in supporting and encouraging others to be assertive?

TRAIT
EIGHT

Trait 8

The Laundry List	The Other Laundry List
We become addicted to excitement.	*We inhibit our fear by staying deadened and numb.*
The Flip Side of The Laundry List	**The Flip Side of The Other Laundry List**
We avoid emotional intoxication and choose workable relationships instead of constant upset.	*We uncover, acknowledge and express our childhood fears and withdraw from emotional intoxication.*

*A*ddiction to excitement may sound like a good thing, but for adult children it takes a very bad turn. We seek out negative excitement – dangerous situations, travel with untrustworthy individuals, and live life precariously – all the while complaining about our circumstances. As children from alcoholic or otherwise dysfunctional families, we received our first doses of excitement very early on, sometimes even *in utero* – before we were born. We were deprived of our innocence as our families struggled with the destructive nature of alcoholism and family dysfunction and the aftermath alcoholism and dysfunction left for the family to clean up. We were thus always in a state of excitement – negative excitement. Tony A. originally wrote that we were addicted to fear, but he thought that the adult children attending the very first ACA meetings would not admit to being fearful. Excitement, he thought, would be easier for them to accept. Negative excitement can come from either being a victim, a victimizer, or a rescuer. In each role, the internal dosing leaves us emotionally intoxicated. Whether at work, home, or even at our meetings, we can conjure up the familiar excitement (fear) we seem to believe is natural. (**The Laundry List**)

ACAs come to meetings because they have hit a bottom, but that bottom is only the beginning of the re-sensitization – the return of feelings. In the Game of Dissociation, we may have used outside substances, a flurry of activities, or a cocktail of internal substances to keep ourselves deadened, numbed, and armored. The result of this was that we felt nothing. The bad news is that we couldn't even have genuinely good feelings beyond the superficial "okay" we would utter when asked. This inhibition eventually stops working for us. Slowly the feelings slip through the cracks of our armor and in our quiet moments we often wonder, "What's wrong with me that I cannot feel?" (**The Other Laundry List**)

As we work the ACA Twelve Steps, reparent ourselves, attend meetings, and process our grief, we begin to see our use of fear as undesirable. We discern the difference between positive and negative excitement and make spiritually conscious decisions to avoid emotional intoxication. Once we have our feelings and buried memories expressed, dosing ourselves with fear or excitement no longer attracts us. In fact, we are repelled by it because it is the life robbing experience of our childhood. Instead, we look for and engage in workable relationships. No longer dissociated or in denial, we accept when a relationship is fraught with constant upset, and we look for life enriching relationships to further our spiritual development. (**The Flip Side of The Laundry List**)

Disinhibiting and freeing the inhibition to our feelings is a very painstaking process that the ACA Steps, reparenting, and ACA meeting attendance make possible. Through the ACA process of recovery, we unearth the hidden childhood fears, we acknowledge our experiences, and we allow ourselves to express our feelings in the safe environment of our meetings, with our fellow travelers and support group. With the support of our ACA family of choice, we can begin to withdraw from the people, activities, and situations that keep us emotionally high, drunk, upset, or otherwise intoxicated. It might feel foreign at first, but eventually we begin to feel rejuvenated and alive – perhaps for the very first time in our life. The freeing up continues as we progress in the program. (**The Flip Side of The Other Laundry List**)

ORIENTATION
Be Prepared to Engage Your Senses

Look at some things (actual)
Make a noise
Eat a peach
Smell some cinnamon
Pat your face

Trait 8 Reflections

Laundry List
We become addicted to excitement.

1. If you could go back to one day of your childhood right now as an invisible person, what level of tension/excitement/fear would you feel?

2. Page 16 of the Fellowship Text states that originally the trait was written as "addicted to fear". Some have defined fear as a distressing emotion aroused by impending danger, evil, pain, etc. Whether the threat is real or imagined, the feeling or condition is of being afraid. Do you relate to this description of fear? Describe in detail what comes up for you while reading the description.

3. List as many factors as you can think of that contributed to the tension in your home.

4. Do you have difficulty doing only one thing at a time? List in detail what you do, if you do more than one thing at a time.

5. Would you describe yourself as someone who frightens easily or is easily excitable? Do you sometimes need to calm down? What do you think this is about in relation to the trait of being addicted to excitement?

6. Do you hate it when your own life is emotionally chaotic, but you still enjoy watching another person's life that is emotionally chaotic?

7. Pay attention to your body, and over time note when you see that your body is tightened from time to time as if you are bracing for an impact. Is your breathing quick and shallow (from your chest) as if you are in a dangerous situation? Do your shoulders rise up and stay that way for no apparent reason? Are your jaws clamped during the day at times? Are your jaws clamped during the night? Do you grind your teeth? Does your body seem to "crave" movement, such as bouncing your knee, tapping your foot or toes, digging around your fingernails, chewing the skin in your mouth or lips, etc.? Compare this to your childhood, do you remember what you did back then physically?

The Other Laundry List
We inhibit our fear by staying deadened and numb.

1. What have you used in your life to inhibit your fears? Describe what you may have used to numb and deaden your experience of life. If you did this as a child, what did you do?

2. Growing up, the people in your life may have displayed inhibition of fear by staying deadened and numb. If so, list in detail who they were and what they did, and how you thought about it when you were young.

3. In your adult life, have you been in relationships with others who display this trait? Describe who they were and what they did, and how you thought about it at that time.

4. Growing up, what fears do you think the people in your life were trying to deaden and numb? As an adult in relationships with others displaying this trait, what fears do you think they were trying to deaden and numb? And finally, for yourself, what fears have you tried to deaden and numb?

5. What is an upside to feeling numb? What is a downside to staying numb? What is an upside for staying deadened? What is a downside for staying deadened? If you had a situation in your life that you survived because of inhibiting your fear by staying deadened and numb, imagine and describe to the best of your ability what might have happened to you if you hadn't been deadened or numbed during this event.

The Flip Side of The Laundry List

We avoid emotional intoxication and choose workable relationships instead of constant upset.

1. Name an experience or type of situation that used to attract you that you choose not to involve yourself in anymore because of the emotional intoxication.

2. Name a type of situation that is still very attractive to you and is usually difficult for you *not* to involve yourself in.

3. Describe in detail your definition of a workable relationship.

4. Describe in detail a relationship you have had that had constant upset.

5. Since coming to ACA are you better able to notice that a relationship might not work for you sooner? If so, describe why this is true.

6. Did the Relationship Worksheet in Step Four of the ACA *Twelve Steps Workbook* help you in this area? If so, how?

7. Did chapter 13 of the Fellowship Text on Relationships help you in this area? If so, how?

The Flip Side of The Other Laundry List

We uncover, acknowledge and express our childhood fears and withdraw from emotional intoxication.

1. Which ACA Steps have helped you uncover and acknowledge your childhood fears?

2. Describe in detail what you have done to express your childhood fears.

3. Before ACA, many adult children were drawn to emotional intoxication. Describe the progression that you've experienced since coming to ACA in relation to withdrawing from emotional intoxication.

4. Which ACA Promises are coming true for you as you uncover, acknowledge, and express your childhood fears and withdraw from emotional intoxication? Describe situations that explain how they are coming true.

TRAIT
NINE

Trait 9

The Laundry List	The Other Laundry List
We confuse love with pity and tend to "love" people who we can "pity" and "rescue".	*We hate people who "play" the victim and beg to be rescued.*
The Flip Side of The Laundry List	**The Flip Side of The Other Laundry List**
We are able to distinguish love from pity, and do not think "rescuing" people we "pity" is an act of love.	*We have compassion for anyone who is trapped in the "drama triangle" and is desperately searching for a way out of insanity.*

*T*he confusion of feelings is a natural by-product of being raised in a family where alcoholism or dysfunctionalism is denied. In our families, the constant conflict of perceptions and realities left us prone to being confused about a great many things. Without our perceptions and realities being validated by an empathetic family, we even have doubt about such fundamental feelings such as love and pity.

As a child, we mimicked our caregivers. We mirrored their emotional, psychological, and spiritual landscape and didn't have the wherewithal to choose or distinguish our feelings. After all, we were babies. We were bound or entranced to our caregivers' relationship patterns out of our natural survival necessity. Clearly in these kinds of families there was, and still may be, an unhealthy dependence. There was a misalignment between the feelings of pity and sympathy on the one hand and compassion and empathy on the other.

In our relationships we relay these mixed signals that we received as children and draw others to us who are equally misaligned. Thus, if we were heroes, we draw people who need rescuing. If we were martyrs, we become involved with lost causes. We do this, all the while thinking and believing we were having healthy relationships with a "normal" share of ups and downs. Still, these misaligned relationships felt unhealthy, unrewarding, and unfulfilling. (**The Laundry List**)

When a child is bombarded with conflicting and confusing messages, the natural tendency is to become psychologically, physically, and spiritually tone deaf or numb. The Game of Dissociation has its benefits. No longer able to bear the weight of such emotional baggage, we strip down our senses to the basic essentials. If anyone even seems like they want to hoist a small packet of "need" on us, we recoil or strike out at their "neediness".

Subconsciously, we may sense that a person's need to be rescued is exactly the same need we buried in the wasteland of our childhood. The accompanying realization of that basic (ontological) loss is too much for us to process or acknowledge. We lash out at them and blame them for being "needy" much the same way we inflicted self-hatred onto our vulnerable True Self, forcing us to take the untenable position of self-sufficiency.

By recycling this dynamic with acquaintances, loved ones, and colleagues, we can unknowingly embrace our ability to stave off our childhood traumas. Yet the resulting psychologically, physically, and spiritually barren person is an inviting oasis to the underwhelmed person. This creates an ecosystem of attraction and repulsion, where both are reenacting a childhood dynamic and each is getting what they subconsciously need to stave off recalling their losses. As a win for the supposed "loser" and a loss for the supposed "winner", this is a lose-lose situation. (**The Other Laundry List**)

Recovery, in this sense, is to be dedicated to achieving clarity by disentangling the confusion. Using the ACA Steps, we can learn to discern between what we were shown and learned as a habit and what we truly believe. When we share at meetings and the space is created to speak our truth, sometimes the internal light may shine suddenly or, like a dimmer switch, may begin to glow a little bit and gradually brighten our insights. We confused love because we were raised in families that were confused about love. We pitied people and called it love because our families showed care and attention toward those they felt sorry for and called it love. In our meetings we don't enable one other, we allow each person to share and create a safe place for all – in essence we say and demonstrate love without pity.

As we take the ACA Steps, we are given an opportunity to release ourselves from the misperceptions and misalignments we were bound to as children, and forge new perceptions and alignments on anvils of patience, tolerance, and acceptance. As we strengthen the atrophied spiritual muscles of discernment, we may find some previously unseen weakness that requires some additional attention, and discover new strengths that deserve an equal measure of celebration. (**The Flip Side of The Other Laundry List**)

As we become more spiritually conscious beings, we become more understanding of our false self and familiar with our True Self. From our emotionally sober True Self, compassion gushes forth and we can see the symbiotic interconnectedness between the "victim" and "victimizer". The interplay between the adrenaline-surged hero or savior, and the melatonin-induced victim or martyr are first realized in us as our True Self emerges and, as we turn our attention outwardly, we can observe these unhealthy dynamics all around us.

Realizing that it was only with God's grace that we were given the humility to find our way to ACA, our peace comes from knowing that somehow, in some miraculous, mysterious way, God will guide those around us when they are ready. No longer compelled to rush into the flames of discord or desperation, we can stand ready for those who might turn to us and ask for help or direction. With a deep sense of gratitude and love, we can share our initial pilgrimage into our family-of-origin work – making a call, searching the internet, reading a book or article, talking with a member of the clergy, or even finding an ACA flier in the street seemingly by coincidence – only to find it was God's invitation to join in this lifetime spiritual quest. **(The Flip Side of The Other Laundry List)**

ORIENTATION
Be Prepared to Engage Your Senses

Look at some things (actual)
Make a noise
Eat a peach
Smell some cinnamon
Pat your face

Trait 9 Reflections

The Laundry List
We confuse love with pity and tend to "love" people who we can "pity" and "rescue".

1. In your past, have you found a "payoff" for "rescuing" a person?

2. In your past, have you found a "payoff" when someone "rescued" you?

3. What is your definition of "confusing love with pity"?

4. When someone shows their interest in you, is there a list of questions that swirl in your mind? If so, please list them.

5. Do you find yourself suspicious when someone shows interest in you? Can you link this reaction to your childhood in some way? If so, please describe in detail.

6. What adult experiences have you had that seem to "document" that when people appear to love you they are actually rescuing, pitying, or displaying some other type of dysfunctional behavior? What happened in one or more of these situations?

7. Is it possible that being raised in an alcoholic/dysfunctional home can create an emptiness in a person who constantly fills this emptiness by "helping" disadvantaged people, the underdog, etc., oblivious as to the reason why?

8. Is it possible that you've attempted to fill an internal emptiness by "helping" others? Are you still doing this today? If so, please describe.

The Other Laundry List

We hate people who "play" the victim and beg to be rescued.

1. Who has annoyed you for getting rescued over and over again? Who has annoyed you for rescuing someone over and over again?

2. What is the reaction you have inside your body when you see this type of "rescuing" situation in progress? What are the thoughts in your mind?

3. When you were a child, did you observe someone playing the victim? Did you observe someone playing the rescuer? Did you wish someone would rescue you? Were you able to appear weak as a child?

4. Did you have to pretend to be strong as a child? Did you feel older than other children your age? Did you look down on them for acting their age? Did you resent them for their "normal" life and being able to be a "normal" child?

5. When watching the news or reading a book or going about your life and you see someone who has success and/or is helped by another, or is number one in their field, or wins the "big prize", do you feel contempt and resentment?

6. Is there a part of you that feels as though life will never be fair to you, and that "the rest of the world" has it "easy" in comparison to your life – that you have endured so much struggle?

7. Have you ever experienced a situation in your life when someone asked for help and "everyone" volunteers to help them, and you feel anger inside for no apparent reason?

8. Do you find it difficult to ask others for help? Do you get mad when others ask for something that you could never ask for? Describe in detail what comes up for you after answering these questions.

The Flip Side of The Laundry List

We are able to distinguish love from pity, and do not think "rescuing" people we "pity" is an act of love.

1. If you have had a desire recently to "rescue" someone who is struggling, describe it here.

2. When you are attending an ACA meeting, are you triggered by this desire to rescue? If so, list why and who and when, etc.

3. Can you list actions coming from love?

4. Which ACA Steps have contributed to your growth in your ability to distinguish love from pity?

5. What do you consider to be the biggest difference between love and pity? In your past, if someone has "rescued" you, did it have negative results for you as a person?

6. Have you been in an ACA meeting and perceived someone acting from a place of "rescuing" or "pitying" or "helping" you? What does that feel like? Please describe in detail.

7. Before ACA, many adult children felt it was helpful to the other person when acting from a place of "rescuing" or "pitying" or "helping". Did you think this way too? Is your thinking different now? If so, please describe in detail.

The Flip Side of The Other Laundry List

We have compassion for anyone who is trapped in the "drama triangle" and is desperately searching for a way out of insanity.

1. Many adult children were unaware that they were repeating similar relationship patterns before coming to ACA. If this is true for you, what have you discovered that you have been doing in relationships that displays some kind of pattern?

2. Is it possible that you saw this pattern as a child and re-enacted it in your own unique way? Please describe in detail.

3. What roles did you see in your childhood as you watched others in their fights and emotional struggles and dramas? Were there any patterns that you saw? Describe in detail who did what, and what roles each played?

4. Do you see others in the world who are in the same trap and do you recognize it "easily"?

5. After reviewing "The Complete Picture" schematic at the beginning of this book, how would you explain the drama triangle to another person?

6. Can you pick a time in your life when you acted out a persecutor, rescuer, or victim aspect of the drama triangle? If so describe it in detail. If you've seen it in others, what did it look like?

7. How have you progressed in ACA in this area? Is there an ACA Promise that is coming true for you in relation to your compassion for others?

TRAIT
TEN

Trait 10

The Laundry List	The Other Laundry List
We have stuffed our feelings from our traumatic childhoods and have lost the ability to feel or express our feelings because it hurts so much (denial).	*We deny that we've been hurt and are suppressing our emotions by the dramatic expression of "pseudo" feelings.*
The Flip Side of The Laundry List	**The Flip Side of The Other Laundry List**
We come out of denial about our traumatic childhoods and regain the ability to feel and express our emotions.	*We accept we were traumatized in childhood and lost the ability to feel. Using the 12 Steps as a program of recovery we regain the ability to feel and remember and become whole human beings who are happy, joyous and free.*

*I*n an effort to deal with our overwhelming and terrorizing childhood experiences (trauma), we learned to "stuff" our feelings. Whether we utilized an internal or external "stuffing", to survive the disruption of our sense of safety we dissociated or disconnected ourselves from our reality and adapted to survive. Sometimes this meant not speaking up because we knew that our families would not be responsive. At other times it might have meant that we used outside substances to help us ignore the feelings. In the Game of Dissociation, we exchanged feeling pain with the relief of not feeling at all. This strategy cost us dearly. In stopping the natural expression of feelings, we also sacrificed our ability to feel or express all of our feelings and became invested in the family denial system. We may have dealt with the overwhelming and terrorizing childhood circumstance, but at what cost? (**The Laundry List**)

One tactic in the Game of Dissociation is to build a life on a false foundation of "resilience". Our imperfect childhoods gave us "strengths". These "strengths" are sometimes noted by others, which reinforces the notion that we found a successful tactic out of our childhood calamities. Over time we may have even been able to speak about our childhoods without any rancor, or to proclaim deep feelings and declare ourselves "finished". Forgiveness, we might have insisted, had been the answer to freeing us from the chains of our childhood experiences. Upon closer inspection, this firmness has some sway. With time the foundation chips away as more of the still unexpressed feelings and memories continue to recycle through our lives. If we are honestly looking at our lives, we might be able to admit that while we did survive, the scars of our childhood experiences still affect us. The unexpressed hurt has nowhere to go. It seems we can neither ignore it nor resolve it unless we first admit it. No longer able to act on the superficial feelings we created to justify our suppression, we find ourself seated with other ACAs, attempting to pull back the layers of denial and wondering how bad the damage has really been. (**The Other Laundry List**)

The ACA Steps and reparenting are extraordinary tools that fit every aspect of the work we do in ACA. While reading ACA literature and attending meetings, we are bound to have both great and small moments of insight. These insights are usually accompanied with memories of one-time fantasies of a well adjusted childhood, but now are reframed as childhood losses. Along with these insights and memories, a well of feelings may come that properly and completely express the hurt. A full remembrance finally frees us from the Game of Dissociation. No longer trying to shut the door, we find the door is opened through God's grace and through our consistently gentle, loving, respectful, and sometimes humorous work. Though coming out of denial and into reality requires persistence, the reward is greater than we could have imagined. Our feelings and perceptions are keener and clearer; our emotional sobriety is purer and longer lasting. What we once considered our plight, is now our delight. Life is worth living once again. (**The Flip Side of The Laundry List**)

Accepting that we were traumatized in childhood results in a total separation from our former belief system that somehow we were unscathed or super resilient. Once off that haughty perch, our descent into our rightful place is made so much the easier through the application of the ACA Steps. As we practice admitting, coming to believe, turning our will and lives over, searching without fear, becoming entirely ready, humility, and listing and making amends, we land on solid ground of the spiritual principles of our program. From here on, our ability to feel deepens. Our ability to recall sharpens, and as we become more integrated, we also find greater integrity within ourselves and with others. There is perhaps no greater gift than to be a whole person after having been fragmented in so many respects throughout all of our lives. The words "happy, joyous, and free" only begin to hint at the rewards. Spiritual awakening and wholeness are equally descriptive, but cannot capture the full breadth of love of life that the work has given us. With our sense of being a part of this extremely powerful and life giving program, we are ready to help the next member who admits they need help and who is willing to accept it. (**The Flip Side of the Other Laundry List**)

ORIENTATION
Be Prepared to Engage Your Senses

Look at some things (actual)
Make a noise
Eat a peach
Smell some cinnamon
Pat your face

Trait 10 Reflections

The Laundry List

We have stuffed our feelings from our traumatic childhoods and have lost the ability to feel or express our feelings because it hurts so much (denial).

1. Which feeling would you say have "stuffed" the deepest? Many adult children find that they fear there are emotions that seem too deeply buried to find, or recover from, or experience safely. Explain how you relate to this sentiment.

2. Have you ever thought that if you allowed your emotions to start coming out that they might never stop? That your life might go downhill really fast? That you could lose total "control" and bad things could happen? Many adult children can't put a name to their emotions; they simply feel an overwhelming sense of confusion and self-doubt. Is any of this true for you? What is true for you?

3. As a child, did you "turn off" your emotions? Did you repeat words or reminders to yourself in order to help you not show an emotion? Did you keep your face from displaying emotions? Did you try to remain neutral in your voice and/or your body posture so as not to show your emotions? Did you hyper-vigilantly study others to see what their emotions were so that you would know how to act? If any of this is true, describe as much as you can in detail.

4. Many adult children say that in their families they were rejected for their emotions so often that they learned to reject their own emotions first, because it hurt so much to be rejected by the adult. The child developed the ability to shut down emotions to the extent of losing touch with feeling any emotions. If this was true for you, describe in detail what was involved in that process for you. If this was not true for you, describe what stuffing your emotions was like for you.

The Other Laundry List

We deny that we've been hurt and are suppressing our emotions by the dramatic expression of "pseudo" feelings.

1. Some adult children experience a sense of low self-esteem and then act super grandiose to cover up their fear of being seen as unimportant. Sometimes they don't even know they're doing it. Have you observed this behavior as a child? Have you observed this behavior in others as an adult? Have you observed this behavior in yourself? Describe any behaviors you have used to cover up some part of you that you were afraid of showing.

2. Describe any situation where you did not show your reaction to someone's "bad" behavior towards you.

3. Why did you hide how you were feeling? Once you were alone, were you able to let your emotions out? If so, what was that like? If you weren't able to express your emotions, what did you do instead?

4. Some adult children have accumulated so many resentments and hurts that they act out in the present day with people who are not responsible for that original damage. Have you done this before? If you have, describe the original damage and the re-enactment in adulthood in as much detail as you can. Why did you do this? What was your motivation? Did you have the thought that you would feel relief? After all was said and done, how did you feel?

5. Write about one person who hurt you. List what they did to you and continue on wherever your pen/pencil/keyboard takes you. Some people enjoy having a scenario conversation out loud rather than writing it down. Either way, find a way that you can use to express your emotions. What are these emotions?

The Flip Side of The Laundry List

We come out of denial about our traumatic childhoods and regain the ability to feel and express our emotions.

1. What ACA Steps and tools have helped you in coming out of denial about your traumatic childhood? Compare your denial before ACA and your self-awareness now.

2. Which ACA Steps and tools have helped you regain the ability to feel and express your emotions? Compare your ability to feel and express your emotions before ACA to where you are today.

3. In this process of coming out of denial, many adult children have ups and downs; what has been your experience?

4. Please describe your process in the following actions with as much detail as you can:

   • feeling your feelings

• expressing your feelings

5. Choose one or more of the ACA Promises that relate to your growth in ACA in coming out of denial, and describe how and what is happening.

The Flip Side of The Other Laundry List

We accept we were traumatized in childhood and lost the ability to feel. Using the 12 Steps as a program of recovery we regain the ability to feel and remember and become whole human beings who are happy, joyous and free.

1. Using the ACA Twelve Steps as a program of recovery, how can we regain the ability to feel and remember and become whole human beings who are happy, joyous, and free?

2. When many members come to ACA, acceptance that they were traumatized is hard to acknowledge before working the ACA Steps and attending meetings, as it takes awhile to accept that the treatment received in childhood was, in fact, trauma. Compare your level of acceptance when starting ACA to your level of acceptance now.

3. How do you think events in your childhood contributed to your losing the ability to feel? Is your ability to feel re-emerging? If so, please describe in detail.

4. Which of the ACA Twelve Steps contributed to your ability to feel and to your awareness of your childhood trauma?

5. Are there any other ACA tools in addition to the ACA Twelve Steps that have helped you? Please list these tools and how they've helped.

6. Using the words "happy, joyous, and free", please describe each level of those states of being in the following life stages:

    a. Your childhood (a specific time or a general description)

        • Happy

        • Joyous

- Free

b. Your pre-ACA adulthood (a specific time or a general description)

- Happy

- Joyous

- Free

c. Yourself as you entered ACA (as a newcomer possibly)

- Happy

- Joyous

- Free

d. Yourself now (today)

- Happy

- Joyous

- Free

TRAIT
ELEVEN

Trait 11

The Laundry List	The Other Laundry List
We judge ourselves harshly and have a very low sense of self-esteem.	*To protect ourselves from self punishment for failing to "save" the family we project our self-hate onto others and punish them instead.*
The Flip Side of The Laundry List	**The Flip Side of The Other Laundry List**
We stop judging and condemning ourselves and discover a sense of self-worth.	*In accepting we were powerless as children to "save" our family we are able to release our self-hate and to stop punishing ourselves and others for not being enough.*

*A*s children we were subjected to extremely difficult conditions which went largely unnoticed. Whether our families were alcoholic or otherwise dysfunctional, chances are that there were few in the family or the community who could see our suffering. As a child, the need to idealize our circumstances left a disconnect between our reality and our fantasy. If we could not be supported in our anger toward our family, that anger had to go somewhere and the only place we could safely place that anger was, ironically, against ourselves.

As we tried to avoid our pain, we became rigid in our views of our conduct and feelings. We figured that the way to avoid the anger of our families was to escape judgment by judging ourselves. The game of dissociating from our feelings gave us safety, but cost us True Self esteem. After all, constant self-criticism means there must be something wrong with merely being. We had tactfully avoided the scorn of our families, but the price we paid was to be hyper-vigilant against any action, behavior, thought or feeling that would reveal our vulnerability or humanness. (**The Laundry List**)

As we grew older, we might have tried to keep the full brunt of our childhood experiences from surfacing, and turned our disappointment and self-hatred onto others. We might have found that others failed to meet our standard. We might have found fault with their clothes, their manner of speaking, how they lived, how they drove – everything and anything that could be criticized was. We took every opportunity to point out flaws and judged them as not being good enough. This undercurrent of criticalness, judgmentalness, and all-or-nothing attack is the belief that, had we been strong enough or good enough, we could have saved our family from alcoholism or dysfunctionalism. If only we had been stronger, wiser, gentler, or smarter, then we could have saved the family.

As a form of grieving, we were stuck in the denial (unfeeling) stage. Denial of our pain became paramount. This "protection" is on its surface designed to make sense of the world around us. However, the net result of such "protection" is that we hurt our True Self and those around us because of the constant barrage of criticism we level on those who are probably as dissociated as we are. The game is completed by our recycling the same unfeeling and uncaring attitude that was embedded in us as children. (**The Other Laundry List**)

We had been preparing to begin this spiritual journey even before learning about ACA. Perhaps it was the constant reminder of our family dynamics or the sudden admission that we were recycling our childhood scenarios. In order to go to an ACA meeting, we had to first stop believing we were guilty. Certainly we could not attend a meeting and feel that we were culpable. No, to make a meeting there had to be a small opening that allowed us to believe that perhaps it wasn't all our doing, that maybe there were contributing factors that led us to the place we found ourself in. In this way, we have been given a gift: the gift of being freed from believing we are condemned to a life of misery. At the same time there is hope: hope that we can get better and have value beyond what our childhood circumstances left us feeling.

This sense of True Self worth may be hard to detect at first, but consistent attendance at meetings allows the feeling to increase until we are strong enough to make a bold step of finding a fellow traveler to work the ACA Steps with. We slowly, gradually yet unmistakably withdraw from the Game of Dissociation. No longer able to deny how we were affected, the memories and feelings are revealed to us over the course of our time in ACA. The promise of who we were meant to be comes into view as we make a commitment to our well being born of True Self esteem. (**The Flip Side of The Laundry List**)

Accepting our inability to "save" the family brings relief from this burden. Like a huge bolder we have been subconsciously carrying, the release of the tension from playing the Game of Dissociation releases the pent up energy that went into keeping the familial weight on our shoulders and back. No longer bound by self-punishment or being a punisher of those around us, we can each feel the freedom to be a person among persons.

We can allow others to be themselves and without our becoming drawn into a Game of Dissociation. We know the Game of Dissociation is full of false self-hatred that impedes our spiritual growth and the spiritual growth of those around us. We have nothing to gain from playing the game. We no longer get ourselves "high" on others' problems or conjure up "issues" to work on. There will be endless opportunities to rejoin the game.

Instead, we choose life. We stand emotionally sober, facing legitimate issues that need to be addressed with the strength of the ACA Twelve Steps, our fellowship, and our fellow travelers. There is no gain from the game. (**The Flip Side of The Other Laundry List**)

ORIENTATION
Be Prepared to Engage Your Senses

Look at some things (actual)
Make a noise
Eat a peach
Smell some cinnamon
Pat your face

Trait 11 Reflections

The Laundry List
We judge ourselves harshly and have a very low sense of self-esteem.

1. Who judged you harshly as a child? Describe who judged you, how they judged you, and how it affected you.

2. Did you observe others being judged in your childhood? Who was getting judged, who was doing the judging, and what was the judging about? Write in detail what happened and how it affected you.

3. Using your imagination, compare your childhood level of self-esteem to the children you saw who you perceived were being raised in loving, "normal" homes. Write in detail how you were affected when you looked at other children and compared them to yourself (if you did that). What types of thoughts went through your mind on a daily basis due to this disparity?

4. Who esteemed you as you grew up? Did anyone esteem you, regard you highly, or value you greatly? Were you able to find this anywhere? Describe who it was and how it affected you. If you had no one esteem you, how do you think this affected you?

5. When you judge yourself harshly (in your worst moments), what is it that you say to yourself? On a day when you are really struggling, describe the way you see yourself in relation to the world. What is your opinion of yourself when presented with an overwhelming problem?

The Other Laundry List

To protect ourselves from self punishment for failing to "save" the family we project our self-hate onto others and punish them instead.

1. When you were little, did you project your hatred onto anyone? If so, please describe all who were involved in this projection of yours. What initiated your actions for feeling this way?

2. Some children project hate as their only way to "fight back". If this was true for you, please describe. If you had a different reason for projecting this hate, please describe it.

3. Were you able to act in an obvious manner, or did you have to hide your punishing of others? Please describe. What did you do as a child to act punitively or to "get back" at someone?

4. How did this projection of self-hate follow you beyond your childhood years? This might be hard to see in yourself – sometimes describing how others do this will jog your memory as to what you might do similarly. Who have you given "pay-backs" to and/or who have you carried a grudge for? This might be a certain "group" of people too.

5. Do you have certain "sneaky" ways of punishing others? Many adult children can hurt a person so stealthily that they can "get back" at someone without "getting caught" by anyone; and if confronted they have an explanation all planned out that will get them "off the hook". Can you describe anything about yourself that might fall into this category?

The Flip Side of The Laundry List
We stop judging and condemning ourselves and discover a sense of self-worth.

1. List any ACA tools that have helped you to stop minimizing, judging, and condemning yourself. Is it true that you are now more tolerant of your own and others' weaknesses? It has been said "mistakes are a sign of growing". If you agree or disagree with this, please comment.

2. Since coming to ACA, how would you say your view of yourself has changed? Has your view of "the world" changed? Has your concept of your parent(s) or caregiver(s) changed? If so, please explain.

3. On a really bad day if you happen to fall into a spiral of self-condemnation, what would help you get back to a realistic view of yourself? If a child sitting beside you was "kicking himself" for a mistake, what might you say to that child?

4. When you came to ACA what were your expectations? What have you gotten so far?

The Flip Side of The Other Laundry List

In accepting we were powerless as children to "save" our family we are able to release our self-hate and to stop punishing ourselves and others for not being enough.

1. What has helped you in ACA to release your self-hate? What has helped you stop punishing yourself? Ask another adult child what has helped them release their self-hate and helped them to stop punishing themselves.

2. Have you noticed that you have less of a desire to punish others? If so, please explain what you have noticed. If you have not, explain what you have noticed.

3. Why were you powerless as a child to "save" your family?

4. Why were you powerless to "make" others treat you well? Were you enough in your family to deserve love and care?

5. Please explain: Are you enough now to deserve love and care? How will you give this to yourself today?

6. What are the loving acts that you give to yourself now? Please explain.

7. If you are punishing yourself and others less, how has this affected your life?

8. How has ACA changed all of your relationships with yourself, your Higher Power, your parents, your loved ones, your working relationships, your "enemies", your ACA acquaintances, etc.?

TRAIT
TWELVE

Trait 12

The Laundry List	The Other Laundry List
We are dependent personalities who are terrified of abandonment and will do anything to hold on to a relationship in order not to experience painful abandonment feelings which we received from living with sick people who were never there emotionally for us.	*We "manage" the massive amount of deprivation we feel, coming from abandonment within the home, by quickly letting go of relationships that threaten our "independence" (not too close).*
The Flip Side of The Laundry List	**The Flip Side of The Other Laundry List**
We grow in independence and are no longer terrified of abandonment. We have interdependent relationships with healthy people, not dependent relationships with people who are emotionally unavailable.	*By accepting and reuniting with the inner child we are no longer threatened by intimacy, by the fear of being engulfed or made invisible.*

*A*s babies, human beings have the longest childhood dependency period of any species. We are dependent on our parents to make us feel safe and accepted. If, as babies, we receive that important nurturing, we can develop naturally and healthfully. If the basic dependency need is not met, we are emotionally, physically, and spiritually abandoned. As adults, we carry this childhood experience to our adult relationships. We subconsciously seek out individuals who are emotionally, physically, and spiritually absent, and insist on staying with the relationship even though we know the relationship is not fulfilling our basic intimacy needs. The mere thought of leaving wracks us with fear – the same fear we experienced as babies looking up to our caregivers and getting everything but love.

This dynamic allows us to remain disconnected from our mates and, just as critically, dissociated from our buried memories and feelings. Constant discord fuels the engine of dissociation by giving us shots of internal drugs. If we are frustrated or angry, we are getting a good dose of adrenaline (an "upper"). If we worry about our mate's well-being, we could be getting a solid dose of endorphins (a "depressant"). If we are depressed, our internal drug of choice may be cortisol or melatonin. With this cocktail of internal drugs, little if any relief from our childhood trauma can be realized. (**The Laundry List**)

Hidden behind our inability to bond with others is a stark truth: we prefer being alone. For us, relationships spell closeness and closeness means pain. The pain of our childhood deprivation, neglect, or abuse is ever present in our interactions with others, and we manage to avoid any close relationships (despite our outward appearance of being sociable) to keep the realization of our childhood pain at bay.

If someone seems nice, we eventually see that they have aspects of their personality that don't match ours. We restrict our circle to only those whose way of interacting with us doesn't cross that invisible emotional wall we have around us to avoid intimacy. Occasionally a person gets through our well-guarded barrier, and gets close enough that we might even think of establishing a genuine relationship. Just as suddenly, we shut them out, because of a real or imagined slight, and reinforce our disconnection from others. We vow never to allow another to come into our world, and thus the disconnection is reinforced.

We declare our independence without realizing we are still imprisoned in our childhood dynamics. The vow of "never again" was probably first a quiet thought as we laid down as children and realized that no one "got us". As adults, we keep our guard up, push back, demean, or otherwise create an atmosphere of fear that blocks any deep connection with others, all the while reinforcing a defensive tactic that speaks to our hidden fears and memories. (**The Other Laundry List**)

With the daily practice of the ACA spiritual principles, we begin to develop our healthy dependence upon our inner loving parent, Inner Child, and our inner Higher Power. As we learn to reparent ourselves through the ups and downs of daily living, we strengthen our bond with our Inner Child. We learn to take our inventory to pull back the veil of denial so that we can witness the return of feelings and memories. The unconscious emotions and memories rise gradually and naturally to the front of our minds, marking our progress.

Allowing these cathartic experiences to happen every so often assures us that the program is working and that our Higher Power is giving us the ability to recall these experiences at the pace Higher Power has determined is best for us. But come they do – and must. It is the expression of these memories and feelings that gives us true independence. When relationships present themselves, we make sure that we are protective of the Inner Child, while also not fearing others unrealistically. We can be an equal partner with others, either as ACA members, fellow travelers, or just by being a member of our communities. No longer wrapped in painful fear, our chosen friendships are easy to entertain and derive wholesome fun from. (**The Flip Side of The Laundry List**)

In ACA we begin with the concept that as children, our True Self went into hiding. We must accept this fact if we are going to heal. We cannot reunite or bond with the Inner Child if we believe that healing is a pipe dream. Once we have accepted the reality of our Inner Child, then there is the process of reuniting with that Inner Child. It is important to note that the Inner Child will not reunite with the inner critical survival parent without the assistance of the inner loving parent.

It is best to be confident that our connection to our inner loving parent is strong, that the inner critical survival parent has been identified, and that we have the support of fellow ACAs to help us make and keep this bond. When we have our Inner Child in the loving and protective embrace of our inner loving parent, we realize that there is nothing "out there" that threatens us "in here". We can be intimate if we choose and not feel that we are being suffocated or ignored. We don't take a dose of the drama of those who would want us to get emotionally (hormonally) high with them. Being emotionally, physically, and spiritually present and visible, we take strides in our spiritual evolution. (**The Flip Side of The Other Laundry List**)

ORIENTATION
Be Prepared to Engage Your Senses

Look at some things (actual)
Make a noise
Eat a peach
Smell some cinnamon
Pat your face

Trait 12 Reflections

The Laundry List

We are dependent personalities who are terrified of abandonment and will do anything to hold on to a relationship in order not to experience painful abandonment feelings which we received from living with sick people who were never there emotionally for us.

1. What do you think "dependent personality" means in reference to this trait? Some adult children have hung on to relationships beyond the point of abuse. Has this been the case for you? If so, please explain in detail why you think this happened.

2. List as many actions and choices you can think of that you've made as a result of your fear of abandonment.

3. What is an example of "doing anything to hold on to a relationship" that you have been involved in? If you've hung on to a relationship beyond the point of abuse, please explain why you think that happened.

4. List some examples of painful abandonment feelings that you experienced in childhood.

5. List some examples of painful abandonment feelings that you've experienced since childhood.

6. How were the people in your childhood "never there emotionally" for you?

7. Who were the "sick" people in your childhood? What types of dysfunction did they act out that you observed?

8. In what ways did you carry on similar dysfunctional actions as those you observed while growing up?

The Other Laundry List

We "manage" the massive amount of deprivation we feel, coming from abandonment within the home, by quickly letting go of relationships that threaten our "independence" (not too close).

1. As a child, how did you manage the deprivation that you felt? Allow yourself to write freely about the feelings that come up as you answer this.

2. Some adult children have dropped relationships at a moment's notice. Has this been the case for you? If so, please explain in detail why you think this happened.

3. Due to your childhood, do you have a strong reaction that involves compulsive thinking when someone shows an interest in you? If so, what types of thoughts go through your mind?

4. Do you suspect a person's motives when they compliment you? When someone shows you common courtesy, do you find yourself wondering why they are doing it? If you find that you are generally suspicious of people, describe why and in what situations it happens the most, with any certain types of people, etc.

The Flip Side of The Laundry List

We grow in independence and are no longer terrified of abandonment. We have interdependent relationships with healthy people, not dependent relationships with people who are emotionally unavailable.

1. Which ACA Steps and other ACA tools have helped you grow in independence?

2. Have you been in a situation where you became aware that your fear of abandonment had weakened?

3. What is your definition of an interdependent relationship?

4. If you are in an interdependent relationship now (not necessarily sexual – any type of relationship), describe what it is like for you and how it is different from a dependent relationship.

5. Describe what experiences you've had in interdependent relationships or what you think an interdependent relationship "might" be like.

6. What is your example of an emotionally unavailable person? Who have you known like this? Have you been emotionally unavailable to others and/or to yourself? In what ways?

7. When a relationship you are in changes or ends, are your reactions inside different now, because of ACA? If so, please describe how.

The Flip Side of The Other Laundry List

By accepting and reuniting with the inner child we are no longer threatened by intimacy, by the fear of being engulfed or made invisible.

1. If someone asked your Inner Child to explain how you accepted and reunited with her/him, what would your Inner Child's answer be? If you have not connected with your Inner Child yet, can you explain your reasons?

2. How have you been threatened by intimacy in your adulthood? Is there a childhood connection that contributes to your feeling threatened by intimacy? If so, please explain.

3. Please describe your thoughts on "fears of being engulfed" in detail.

4. Do you have any idea why "fears of being engulfed" is something that some adult children experience? If it is something that you've experienced, please explain where you think it came from and what it has been like to live with that fear throughout your life.

5. List some instances where you felt you were invisible. Nowadays, what can you do to ensure you do not "become" invisible in a relationship?

6. How is it that two people can cooperate to get their needs met? Can you describe an example?

7. Which ACA Promise do you relate to by accepting and reuniting with your Inner Child?

TRAIT THIRTEEN

Trait 13

The Laundry List	The Other Laundry List
Alcoholism is a family disease and we became para-alcoholics and took on the characteristics of the disease even though we did not pick up the drink.	*We refuse to admit we've been affected by family dysfunction or that there was dysfunction in the home or that we have internalized any of the family's destructive attitudes and behaviors.*
The Flip Side of The Laundry List	**The Flip Side of The Other Laundry List**
The characteristics of alcoholism and para-alcoholism we have internalized are identified, acknowledged, and removed.	*By acknowledging the reality of family dysfunction we no longer have to act as if nothing were wrong or keep denying that we are still unconsciously reacting to childhood harm and injury.*

*A*nyone who was raised in an alcoholic home knows that the alcoholic affected everyone in the family. In this trait, however, we are also told that the entire family is affected by the disease. How can this be? I don't drink – how can I be affected? The second part of this trait spells out the affect: para-alcoholism. When Tony A. wrote "para-alcoholism", he was trying to convey that we were like the alcoholic. In the years since, our experience has shown us that we aren't "like an alcoholic", we are internal addicts just as dependent on the inside drugs as the alcoholic is on the outside substance. In fact, the alcoholic was an internal addict first, then she/he picked up the outside substance. Thus, the characteristics of the alcoholic are the same as the characteristics of the internal addict.

These characteristics were passed on and we acquired them as defenseless children. Whether we chose to drink or use other substances, the core of our being is consumed by addictive attitudes and behaviors. We can easily substitute one substance or behavior for another and keep using the Game of Dissociation to deny the full remembrance of our traumatic childhood experiences. (**The Laundry List**)

Refusing to admit that we have been affected is more damaging to us than merely denying that we or our family have been affected. Refusal is the use of the will to resist. Thus entrenched, any hint of the impact of addiction on our childhoods can be met with strong opposition and a wide range of defenses, some of which can be quite fierce. After all, this admission can mean that everything we have built our lives on has been a falsehood. We might point to our homes, our children, and our careers as testimonials of having found our way. Yet the gnawing question is, "If we are so well-adjusted, then why do we feel so empty that it brings us to these meetings?"

If we look carefully at **The Laundry List** and **The Other Laundry List** traits and do not find anything in them that catches our attention, then perhaps we are not adult children. Indeed this would be a most miraculous result. However, if we are honest, as we survey our lives and consider these lists, it is a rare person who can claim to have survived such experiences without scars that affect other aspects of their lives. (**The Other Laundry List**)

Attending and sharing at meetings, reading ACA literature, and working with a fellow traveler allows the natural and gentle unburdening of unprocessed hurt or grief to occur. The discomfort is identified through consistent work of the ACA Steps. As we acknowledge the effect, the removal of the sting of our childhood experiences becomes less and less. We might even find some of our recollections to be humorous. Our tears of sadness eventually turn to tears of laughter as we begin to realize that the gift of recovery has come into our lives.

As we keep coming to meetings, the Power that brings us to the rooms of ACA reveals the tender love available to us as a result of having such harrowing experiences so that we can have a magnificent ascent to spiritual consciousness. As the retrieval and removal work continues, we are amazed at the gifts we receive. Clarity, insight, and the ability to express unprocessed grief are some of the benefits of working the ACA program. We realize our Higher Power holds us in a tender embrace, allowing us to know the unconditional love of the True Self, of inner Higher Power, Inner Child(ren) and our fellow ACA members. (**The Flip Side of The Laundry List**)

As we work the program, our denial eventually turns to acceptance. Our admission that we were affected starts a chain of events that leads us to deeper acknowledgments about our excuses for our contorted world view. In the process we begin to admit that things aren't always right and that we are unconsciously reacting to childhood harms that went unacknowledged in the past. Our injury, our losses, and our grief finally have an opportunity to be released. The joy of living life becomes a reality. Even though we once thought we were living the best lives we could imagine, now our Higher Power opens the blinds, letting new light into our world and shining love wherever we look.

Even the newcomer's resistance is appreciated as the first stage of ACA work. No longer caught in the false self bind, we can empathize without feeling compelled to rescue. We realize that Higher Power is in charge and guiding newcomers the way we were guided – with love and patience. We share about our continuing spiritual awakening – not solely for the benefit it may give others, but more importantly – because it reinforces and furthers our own spiritual consciousness. We are alive! We are truly alive! (**The Flip Side of The Other Laundry List**)

ORIENTATION
Be Prepared to Engage Your Senses

Look at some things (actual)
Make a noise
Eat a peach
Smell some cinnamon
Pat your face

Trait 13 Reflections

The Laundry List

Alcoholism is a family disease and we became para-alcoholics and took on the characteristics of the disease even though we did not pick up the drink.

1. How would you define para-alcoholism? How would you define the characteristics of the disease of alcoholism? Which was it for you; did you pick up the drink, or did you *not* pick up the drink? Can you explain this in detail?

2. Were there any family members who were not affected by the characteristics of the family disease? If so, please list them and how they were different, and why you think they were different. If, in your situation, all members were affected, how does that reality make you feel about them, about yourself, etc.?

3. You may not have picked up the drink and you may have picked up the drink, but you may have picked up something else. Please list anything that you picked up as a result of being raised in an alcoholic/dysfunctional family. This can include behaviors, compulsions, items, substances, etc.

4. Using your definition of para-alcoholism, would you describe your parent(s) or caregiver(s) as para-alcoholics?

5. List in detail examples of distorted thinking and fears that you have, from being raised in an alcoholic/dysfunctional family.

The Other Laundry List

We refuse to admit we've been affected by family dysfunction or that there was dysfunction in the home or that we have internalized any of the family's destructive attitudes and behaviors.

1. Have you and/or your other family members ever minimized the difficulty of your childhood? If so, please list what has been said by you or others. Why do you think you or others have minimized in this way?

2. Have you ever thought any "someday when" types of thoughts such as '*If* _____ *changes, I'll be happy*'? If so, please make a list of these "someday" thoughts.

3. Many adult children don't understand that they have these inside effects, and come to hate themselves and/or are confused about why outside circumstances in life aren't helping to make them finally feel happy or "normal". Not knowing that the issue is inside, they often blame themselves for not being happy. Has this been the case for you? Please explain in detail.

4. What are some of the hardest-to-admit destructive attitudes and behaviors that you have internalized?

The Flip Side of The Laundry List

The characteristics of alcoholism and para-alcoholism we have internalized are identified, acknowledged, and removed.

1. Which ACA Steps and tools have helped you in *identifying* your characteristics of alcoholism and para-alcoholism?

2. Which ACA Steps and tools have helped you in *acknowledging* your characteristics of alcoholism and para-alcoholism?

3. What ACA Steps and tools have helped you in *removing* your characteristics of alcoholism and para-alcoholism?

4. What characteristics are you aware of that are still present and causing you pain from time to time? Before you got to ACA, was your life different than it is now? If so, please write in detail.

The Flip Side of The Other Laundry List

By acknowledging the reality of family dysfunction we no longer have to act as if nothing were wrong or keep denying that we are still unconsciously reacting to childhood harm and injury.

1. Which ACA Promises are coming true because of this growth you've had in acknowledging the reality of family dysfunction?

2. Make a list of some ACA slogans (see Fellowship Text p. 52) that can help support you in times when you might be reacting to childhood harm and injury. Elaborate on why you selected them.

3. List situations where you are more likely to act as if nothing is wrong with you. List people or types of people and places where this desire to "act okay" causes you to struggle most.

4. Describe in detail what you consider to be the differences between acting consciously and reacting unconsciously.

TRAIT
FOURTEEN

Trait 14

The Laundry List	The Other Laundry List
Para-alcoholics are reactors rather than actors.	*We act as if we are nothing like the dependent people who raised us.*
The Flip Side of The Laundry List	**The Flip Side of The Other Laundry List**
We are actors, not reactors.	*We stop denying and do something about our post-traumatic dependency on substances, people, places and things to distort and avoid reality.*

*T*he term para-alcoholic is meant to suggest that as children we adopted or adapted a belief and behavioral system that parallels the alcoholic. In the years since, we have learned that the belief system and behavioral patterns are not "like" (para) an alcoholic but are indeed the same as the alcoholic. The non-drinking member of the alcoholic family system is governed by the same internal biochemical and psychological disposition that ultimately leads to alcoholism, addiction, and unhealthy dependence. Viewed in this light, adult children are equally dependent on the chaos, upset, excitement, and fear as the alcoholic is to the alcohol, drugs, or behaviors. In fact, these attitudes and dispositions are a precursor to becoming an alcoholic or addict.

Clearly, the alcoholic or addict is first addicted to these internal biochemical and psychological attitudes and disposition, and this leads to the use of outside substances as an add on to the already primed system.

The reactive quality that we can easily see in the alcoholic's behavior is just as evident in the non-drinking member of the alcoholic family system; although not as socially stigmatized as the stumbling alcoholic or the drug addict, it is just as intoxicating and life draining. Our primary addictive reactions are our "high", no matter how socially acceptable or righteous, and it is as progressive and deadly as a secondary addiction to alcohol, drugs, and other addictive behaviors. Whether we are enabling or acting like a hero, our "role" in the Game of Dissociation rewards us by not allowing us to feel the pain of being emotionally, physically, and spiritually hurt. (**The Laundry List**)

While we can more easily admit that our families may have been unhealthy, we usually have an escape in denial: "It didn't affect me." We act differently; we are responsible, well adjusted, model employees, and productive members of our society. This third act completely conceals the first and second act of this classic family tragedy. Without the expression of the buried hurt along with the memories they are attached to, our lives feel shallow and superficial. Our relationships are guarded. We are overly sensitive to people's words and actions. The role in this act is a difficult one that requires a great deal of emotional, physical, and psychic energy to keep the reality of our childhood experiences at a safe distance. The transfer of our family's dysfunction is fused with our being, even if we insist that it doesn't exist. Denial and distinction does not erase the plain fact that the apple and the tree are so closely connected. As social beings, we are bound to our family system from our need to belong, and if belonging means survival, we hold onto that bond with all our might until one day it occurs to us that the bond may be affecting our well-being.

The Game of Dissociation can last a lifetime or it can become dismantled slowly over a span of days or months when we start to see how we are dosing ourselves by indulging in superiority – intellectual escapism – self-righteous disdain for our fellow human beings. All of these perspectives are quite common and celebrated in a culture rich with critical absent-mindedness. We might strike out on our own, and feel that putting distance and some semblance of normalcy into our lives has severed the link. However, no matter where we go, there we are, finding another unhealthy dependence just like the one we grew up knowing best. We can run, but the addiction lurks in our subconscious, looking for the opportunity to numb us to the extraordinary burden of our heavy spirits. (**The Other Laundry List**)

The freedom of choice is rarely given freely. The work we do by attending meetings, taking the ACA Steps, doing service, connecting with our inner loving parent, getting in touch with our Inner Child, facing our inner critical survival parent, working with fellow travelers – yes, it is a lot of work – and we do it to achieve the freedom to choose how we respond to life versus reacting to it. In the heat of the moment, many of us will still react. However, we then take time later on to use the tools of recovery. We better understand the sequence of events, the part we played, and the possible alternative choices we could have made, and make a note to try it differently the next time we find ourselves in the same situation. As human beings, we are likely to make many mistakes.

Now, when we make a mistake, we have tools that show us some of the ways we can correct our human foibles. No longer dragged into the Game of Dissociation, we can release ourselves from the reactive qualities and stop the internal biochemical rush we previously thought was desirable. We now have keen awareness of these internal drugs as poisonous to our new way of life, and we take a healthy stand for living life without the use of this internal addiction. We simply walk away from the Game of Dissociation. The life we were meant to live awaits us, and we steady our gaze on our spiritual consciousness, and integration, and move forward. (**The Flip Side of The Laundry List**)

Resistance to the program is continuous, but through our consistent effort, the support of our fellowship, and with the grace of our Higher Power, we have stopped denying that we are recreating and recycling our learned reactions to being raised in a terrorized family system. The work of disentangling the numerous ways we are bound by unhealthy dependence on the "stand-ins" of substances, people, places, and things is exhilarating – in a positive, spiritual way that without ACA would have caused us frustration and confusion. Led by the ACA Steps to deeper consciousness, we receive daily opportunities for spiritual growth and evolution. Our perceptions are less clouded by our past, and the authentic experiences that are presented in our daily lives are greeted by healthy, appropriate, and precise actions to be worked through instead of avoided. The road ahead of us has many curves, valleys, and tunnels. We slow down our speed to maneuver them graciously, knowing the Higher Power is only asking us to do what we need to do to advance our spiritual consciousness. Instead of playing the Game of Dissociation, we take our place in this world as vibrant lovers of life. (**The Flip Side of The Laundry List**)

ORIENTATION
Be Prepared to Engage Your Senses

Look at some things (actual)
Make a noise
Eat a peach
Smell some cinnamon
Pat your face

Trait 14 Reflections

The Laundry List
Para-alcoholics are reactors rather than actors.

1. Some people use the term "knee-jerk reaction" to describe something a person does automatically, as if on reflex. Would you say that you have some of these knee-jerk reactions that you've noticed? Please list them, and circle the ones that you remember other family members expressing.

2. Some adult children have said "that person knows how to push my buttons" to describe one person's ability to affect another. Sometimes the inference is that the person "pushing" the buttons knows what they are doing and they are doing it purposely. Have you said this in your life? Have you heard others say it? Do you feel that people are able to cause a reaction in you depending on what they say or do? Do you feel in some cases that these people are doing it on purpose? If so, please explain in detail what you mean.

3. Please explain if you experience times when it seems you have no choice other than to react in the way you're reacting – as if there is an internal switch that turns on and you couldn't turn it off even if you tried. Describe in detail if you relate to this happening at any time in your life.

4. When you were a child, did you observe people reacting off of each other? If so, describe some scenarios where this happened.

5. Describe how, in your adult life today, you've automatically reacted to others. How does this relate to the reactions of family members you observed long ago.

The Other Laundry List

We act as if we are nothing like the dependent people who raised us.

1. Have you heard anyone say anything like "my childhood was horrible, but I've left all that behind me now"? And if so, what is your opinion of that reality now that you've come to ACA?

2. Some adult children can easily point out the faults in other people, but seem unable to see faults within themselves. Does this appear to be true with you? If so, please list some examples.

3. Describe a "dependent person". For some adult children, being seen as a dependent person causes fear, and sometimes anger and rage. When you were a child, was there a high price to pay if someone viewed you as dependent? What happened in your childhood when someone was seen as dependent?

4. It's been observed that adult children can be chameleon-like in their ability to adapt to a situation or person for survival's sake. Is this true for you? Have you role-played a different personality to survive? If so, please list in detail the skills at adapting that you've used in your life, including ways you adapted in childhood. Include why you felt the need to make these adaptations in each scenario.

The Flip Side of The Laundry List

We are actors, not reactors.

1. Since coming to ACA are you more aware on occasion that there are choices available when it comes to your possible actions? If so, please explain. If not, please list the types of people or situations where it is harder for you to act instead of react.

2. Which ACA Steps and tools have helped you move from reacting to acting?

3. When you live life as an actor, what are the results you've noticed? When you live life as a reactor what are the results that you've noticed?

4. Would you have survived your childhood if you were not a reactor? What would have happened if you had not become a reactor in order to survive?

The Flip Side of The Other Laundry List

We stop denying and do something about our post-traumatic dependency on substances, people, places and things to distort and avoid reality.

1. Which ACA Steps and tools have helped you to relieve your post-traumatic dependency on using:

    • Substances to distort and avoid reality.

    • People to distort and avoid reality.

    • Places to distort and avoid reality.

    • Things to distort and avoid reality.

2. Which parts of the ACA Solution are coming true for you as you stop denying and do something about post-traumatic dependency?

3. What helped you stop denying that you had post-traumatic dependencies?

4. What tools in the ACA program help you the most to stay in the present as opposed to acting from the past patterns from childhood?

APPENDICES

THE COMPLETE PICTURE
Characteristics of an Adult Child

The Laundry List

1) We became isolated and afraid of people and authority figures.

2) We became approval seekers and lost our identity in the process.

3) We are frightened by angry people and any personal criticism.

4) We either become alcoholics, marry them or both, or find another compulsive personality such as a workaholic to fulfill our sick abandonment needs.

5) We live life from the viewpoint of victims and we are attracted by that weakness in our love and friendship relationships.

6) We have an overdeveloped sense of responsibility and it is easier for us to be concerned with others rather than ourselves. This enables us not to look too closely at our own faults.

7) We get guilt feelings when we stand up for ourselves instead of giving in to others.

8) We become addicted to excitement.

9) We confuse love with pity and tend to "love" people who we can "pity" and "rescue".

10) We have stuffed our feelings from our traumatic childhoods and have lost the ability to feel or express our feelings because it hurts so much (denial).

11) We judge ourselves harshly and have a very low sense of self-esteem.

12) We are dependent personalities who are terrified of abandonment and will do anything to hold on to a relationship in order not to experience painful abandonment feelings which we received from living with sick people who were never there emotionally for us.

13) Alcoholism is a family disease and we became para-alcoholics and took on the characteristics of the disease even though we did not pick up the drink.

14) Para-alcoholics are reactors rather than actors.

Victim / Rescuer I

Unintegrated and

In the "Game" of Dissociation these positions are receivers of insult & injury* delivered by dissociative dosing transactions.

Completing the Cycle of Violence
Closing the Circle
Positions in The Game of Dissociation

Male Victim • Overt Victim • Covert Victimizer	Female Victim • Overt Victim • Covert Victimizer
Male Victimizer • Overt Victimizer • Covert Victim	Female Victimizer • Overt Victimizer • Covert Victim

↕   ↕

The Apprentice / The Child **

Bringing the Family Drama to a Close
(Withdrawing from The Game of Dissociation)

Persecutor   Rescuer Type I & II

Victim

The Drama Triangle*

Victim

Rescuer Type I & II   Sober Side of the Self

Persecutor

A Fourth Possibility

Characteristics of an Integrated Person

The Flip Side of The Laundry List

1) We move out of isolation and are not unrealistically afraid of other people, even authority figures.

2) We do not depend on others to tell us who we are.

3) We are not automatically frightened by angry people and no longer regard personal criticism as a threat.

4) We do not have a compulsive need to recreate abandonment.

5) We stop living life from the standpoint of victims and are not attracted by this trait in our important relationships.

6) We do not use enabling as a way to avoid looking at our own shortcomings.

7) We do not feel guilty when we stand up for ourselves.

8) We avoid emotional intoxication and choose workable relationships instead of constant upset.

9) We are able to distinguish love from pity, and do not think "rescuing" people we "pity" is an act of love.

10) We come out of denial about our traumatic childhoods and regain the ability to feel and express our emotions.

11) We stop judging and condemning ourselves and discover a sense of self-worth.

12) We grow in independence and are no longer terrified of abandonment. We have interdependent relationships with healthy people, not dependent relationships with people who are emotionally unavailable.

13) The characteristics of alcoholism and para-alcoholism we have internalized are identified, acknowledged, and removed.

14) We are actors, not reactors.

---

* Note: Insult and Injury = Punishment, abandonment, conditional acceptance, conditional care
** "Oh, No! These are my choices?"
*** Following Karpman 1967, 2007

For an explanation of the roles and transactions in the "Game" of Dissociation, see p. 155.

The Other Laundry List / The Opposite Laundry List
(A reaction Formation List; "It Will Never Happen To Me")

1) To cover our fear of people and our dread of isolation we tragically become the very authority figures who frighten others and cause them to withdraw.
2) To avoid becoming enmeshed and entangled with other people and losing ourselves in the process, we become rigidly self-sufficient. We disdain the approval of others.
3) We frighten people with our anger and threat of belittling criticism.
4) We dominate others and abandon them before they can abandon us or we avoid relationships with dependent people altogether. To avoid being hurt, we isolate and dissociate and thereby abandon ourselves.
5) We live life from the standpoint of a victimizer, and are attracted to people we can manipulate and control in our important relationships.
6) We are irresponsible and self-centered. Our inflated sense of self-worth and self-importance prevents us from seeing our deficiencies and shortcomings.
7) We make others feel guilty when they attempt to assert themselves.
8) We inhibit our fear by staying deadened and numb.
9) We hate people who "play" the victim and beg to be rescued.
10) We deny that we've been hurt and are suppressing our emotions by the dramatic expression of "pseudo" feelings.
11) To protect ourselves from self punishment for failing to "save" the family we project our self-hate onto others and punish them instead.
12) We "manage" the massive amount of deprivation we feel, coming from abandonment within the home, by quickly letting go of relationships that threaten our "independence" (not too close).
13) We refuse to admit we've been affected by family dysfunction or that there was dysfunction in the home or that we have internalized any of the family's destructive attitudes and behaviors.
14) We act as if we are nothing like the dependent people who raised us.

emotionally intoxicated

Rescuer II / Persecutor

In the "Game" of Dissociation these positions are givers of insult & injury* delivered by dissociative dosing transactions.

Completing the Recovery Process

Rescuer Type I & II | Victim | Persecutor | Sober Side of the Self

Whole, healthy, sane & safe

The Sober Self

The Flip Side of The Other Laundry List

1) We face and resolve our fear of people and our dread of isolation and stop intimidating others with our power and position.
2) We realize the sanctuary we have built to protect the frightened and injured child within has become a prison and we become willing to risk moving out of isolation.
3) With our renewed sense of self-worth and self-esteem we realize it is no longer necessary to protect ourselves by intimidating others with contempt, ridicule and anger.
4) We accept and comfort the isolated and hurt inner child we have abandoned and disavowed and thereby end the need to act out our fears of enmeshment and abandonment with other people.
5) Because we are whole and complete we no longer try to control others through manipulation and force and bind them to us with fear in order to avoid feeling isolated and alone.
6) Through our in-depth inventory we discover our true identity as capable, worthwhile people. By asking to have our shortcomings removed we are freed from the burden of inferiority and grandiosity.
7) We support and encourage others in their efforts to be assertive.
8) We uncover, acknowledge and express our childhood fears and withdraw from emotional intoxication.
9) We have compassion for anyone who is trapped in the "drama triangle" and is desperately searching for a way out of insanity.
10) We accept we were traumatized in childhood and lost the ability to feel. Using the 12 Steps as a program of recovery we regain the ability to feel and remember and become whole human beings who are happy, joyous and free.
11) In accepting we were powerless as children to "save" our family we are able to release our self-hate and to stop punishing ourselves and others for not being enough.
12) By accepting and reuniting with the inner child we are no longer threatened by intimacy, by the fear of being engulfed or made invisible.
13) By acknowledging the reality of family dysfunction we no longer have to act as if nothing were wrong or keep denying that we are still unconsciously reacting to childhood harm and injury.
14) We stop denying and do something about our post-traumatic dependency on substances, people, places and things to distort and avoid reality.

Appendix A

Completing the Circle (in the Cycle of Violence)

*T*o understand how the Cycle of Family Violence is transmitted (from parents to children) it is necessary to **identify and delineate all of the components** of the inter-generational transfer of traumatically generated internal addiction and emotional intoxication.

These are:

> **repetition of dialogue** (self talk and self recrimination),
> **re-creation of scenes** (the symbolic movies in the mind) **and situations** (with real-time "stand-ins" – the "Replacements") which together can be called **"The Distractors"**,
> **the recapitulation of emotions** (feels the same) through the reconstitution of the biochemistry (internal uppers, downers, pain-killers and thought regulators) and **reconfiguration of the body** (held the same way), all of which is called the *process of traumatic reproduction*. (Freud/Ferenczi)[1, 2].

This results in a **predictable, dissociative forgetting that leaves a person numb, unconscious, and stuck in the past**.

Children who are caught up in the frightening, erratic, chaotic and demoralizing environment of a severely dysfunctional family are constantly searching for clues and indicators as to what their highly conditional "providers" demand and will tolerate in meeting the basic needs of the children. The children have no way of knowing that their caregivers themselves are relying on a confusing, hurtful, "superstitious" mix of sane and insane behaviors and beliefs about survival that was passed on to them. The beat goes on with one generation pounding its insanity into the next. In order not to go completely mad children have to dissociate or partially separate from their unbearable reality. **The dilemma of dissociation is that traumatized people can't afford to forget what they do <u>not</u> want to remember.**

The memories of early trauma experiences represent how the world was, who to fear, and what must be done to maintain some degree of safety. Therefore, early trauma memories and emotions are always threatening to break through into consciousness. A dissociated person is preoccupied with dividing energy and attention into maintaining dissociation and attempting to live some kind of meaningful life in the present.

The Problem says we are "dependent personalities" who are "terrified of abandonment", and will "do almost anything to hold on to a relationship in order not to be abandoned emotionally". However we keep "choosing insecure relationships because they 'match' our childhood relationship with alcoholic or dysfunctional parents." **The "almost anything" we will do is to hold on to the "package deal" of dissociative living we were given in childhood in the not unreasonable**

1 Freud, Sigmund, *The Basic Writings of Sigmund Freud*, New York: Random House, 1995
2 Ferenczi, Sándor, *The Clinical Diary of Sándor Ferenczi*, Cambridge: Harvard University Press, 1988

belief that this is the best we can do. The form of the package deal follows Eric Berne's life game of "alcoholic"[3]. However, for adult children, Berne's variation of "dry drunk" is the best fit. As in all of Berne's games there are a series of moves (transactions) by the players that result in a "payoff".

In the "Game" of Dissociation[4] there are two basic positions, victim and victimizer (persecutor). The victim may have a confederate, the earnest, "helpful", ineffective rescuing friend or pal (Type I Rescuer). The Type I Rescuer is essentially a victim waiting to happen.

The persecutor may be disguised as a highly conditional rescuer – "I'll 'accept', 'love' you if and when" (Type II Rescuer). Of course the conditions can never be met and the Type II Rescuer can flip into the persecutor at the drop of a hat.

The persecutor is the one who gives the insults and injuries that maintain dissociation (dissociative dosing transactions) while the victim is the one who does the receiving.

A "successful" dosing transaction is one in which the insult and injury exchange leaves both (or all) the players in the game more absent than present (unconscious – stupefied) and more *there then* (regressed) than *here now*. In other words, dissociated (hypoxic, hypercarbic, hypoglycemic).

Both victim and persecutor are terrified of abandonment. The victim is more obviously desperate and needy while the persecutor is so terrified of falling into the abyss of abandonment that the terror has been completely walled off. The only form of love or connection that can be tolerated is to be the one who punishes and abandons, not to be the one who is punished, neglected and finally abandoned.

Children don't know they are targeted to become objects of addiction in the "Game" of Dissociation, that the adults will overtly and covertly force the children to accept (introject) their demands that they embrace the addict way of life. To put it bluntly, the demand from adults to children in a conflict-addicted family is "we need you to be a player (addict) to cope with and endure our hyper-dependency syndrome". The forced introjection is the means – whereby the "Game" of Dissociation is transmitted intergenerationally along with the twisted, superstitious justification/ rationale for continuing the family's insanity.

The solution is to use the Twelve Steps to eject the introjects and stop the "game", to regain personal integrity, to become sober and sane. The essential point is the traumatic etiology of addiction – stop the trauma / re-trauma; stop the dissociation / addiction. The word addiction comes from the Latin "to say to", to say yes to a strong habit (denial). Essentially recovery is a matter of turning that around and just saying "No!"

3 Berne, Eric, *Games People Play*, New York: Ballantine Books, 1992
4 "Obedience to Insanity: Social Collusion in the Creation and Maintenance of Dissociative States": 1989, M. R. Smith (initial description of the "Game" of Dissociation)
   "Completing the Circle in the Cycle of Violence: Covert and Overt Victims and Victimizers" (22nd Annual ACA Convention)

Appendix B

Sample Opening Script for "4x4" Meeting

Set Up – refer the participants to the following:

• **Reading excerpt: The Laundry List – Problem**
  If using the *ACA Fellowship Text (BRB)*, see Chapter 1 on pp. 3-4, 8-9, and pp. 10-18.
  If using *The Laundry Lists Workbook*, see Appendix C beginning on p. 160.

• **The week's corresponding trait.**
  Page numbers for the traits are listed for both the *ACA Fellowship Text (BRB)* and *The Laundry Lists Workbook*. Refer to the page numbers in the book you are using.

(Meeting Days and Times)

Good evening, we would like to start the meeting. We ask that all cell phones be turned off. We open the meeting with the ACA Serenity Prayer.

My name is _____, I am a recovering adult child. Welcome to The ACA 4x4 meeting where we focus on the four Laundry Lists, four traits at a time. By identifying with the Laundry Lists traits, we can begin a recovery process of taking the suggested ACA Twelve Steps to integrate the traits, to reparent ourselves to wholeness with gentleness, humor, love, and respect, and to awaken spiritually.

This week we are on Trait #___ and the traits are (CHAIRPERSON read out the four traits from the traits table).

We will take turns reading one or two paragraphs of the *ACA Fellowship Text (BRB)* excerpt or *The Laundry Lists Workbook (LLWB)* excerpt and the reading about Trait #___ on page*___. (CHAIRPERSON announce the page for the trait we are covering from the lists on the following page.)

If using *The Laundry Lists Workbook*, the traits can be found on the following pages:

*Trait 1 – p. 1	Trait 2 – p. 11	Trait 3 – p. 21
Trait 4 – p. 31	Trait 5 – p. 41	Trait 6 – p. 51
Trait 7 – p. 65	Trait 8 – p. 75	Trait 9 – p. 85
Trait 10 – p. 97	Trait 11 – p. 109	Trait 12 – p. 119
Trait 13 – p. 131	Trait 14 – p. 141	

If using the *ACA Fellowship Text (BRB)*, the traits can be found on the following pages:

*Trait 1 – p. 10	Trait 2 – p. 11	Trait 3 – p. 11
Trait 4 – p. 12	Trait 5 – p. 14	Trait 6 – p. 14
Trait 7 – p. 15	Trait 8 – p. 16	Trait 9 – p. 12
Trait 10 – p. 17	Trait 11 – p. 15	Trait 12 – p. 17
Trait 13 – p. 12	Trait 14 – p. 17	

May I have someone please start the reading? (CHAIRPERSON STOP.)

(CHAIRPERSON After the reading is finished.)

Thank you all for reading.

A few words about sharing at this meeting: This is a safe place to share our childhood experiences and their effects on us today without judgment or criticism. We encourage each member to share openly about her or his experiences. By regularly sharing in ACA meetings, we find we start to come out of our denial and gain freedom from the effects of alcoholism or family dysfunction.

In ACA we do not cross talk. Cross talk means interrupting, referring to, or commenting on what another person has said during the meeting. We do this because when we were growing up, no one listened to us or they told us our feelings were wrong. We accept what others say because it is true for them.

We encourage you to not touch, hug, or attempt to comfort others if they become emotional or cry during an ACA meeting. We allow the person to feel his or her feelings without interrupting their process.

Our group's conscience has decided to have a lead of up to 10 minutes followed by four-minute timed shares from the floor. Our Spiritual Timekeeper will give the leader and the sharers a "One Minute" signal and "Time" signal. Please wrap up your share when the "Time" signal is given. The sharing will end at 5 minutes before the end of meeting.

Would someone like to volunteer to be our Spiritual Timekeeper? Thanks.

We have asked _____ to share, and then the floor will be open for sharing popcorn style. Now I give you _____. (CHAIRPERSON STOP.)

(CHAIRPERSON after the lead.)

Thank you for sharing.

For those who may have joined us late, we are on Trait #___. We read about Trait #___ that is on page*___, and the Traits for this week and the traits are (CHAIRPERSON read out the four traits from the traits table).

If using *The Laundry Lists Workbook*, the traits can be found on the following pages:

*Trait 1 – p. 1	Trait 2 – p. 11	Trait 3 – p. 21
Trait 4 – p. 31	Trait 5 – p. 41	Trait 6 – p. 51
Trait 7 – p. 65	Trait 8 – p. 75	Trait 9 – p. 85
Trait 10 – p. 97	Trait 11 – p. 109	Trait 12 – p. 119
Trait 13 – p. 131	Trait 14 – p. 141	

If using the *ACA Fellowship Text (BRB)*, the traits can be found on the following pages:

*Trait 1 – p. 10	Trait 2 – p. 11	Trait 3 – p. 11
Trait 4 – p. 12	Trait 5 – p. 14	Trait 6 – p. 14
Trait 7 – p. 15	Trait 8 – p. 16	Trait 9 – p. 12
Trait 10 – p. 17	Trait 11 – p. 15	Trait 12 – p. 17
Trait 13 – p. 12	Trait 14 – p. 17	

The floor is open for sharing popcorn style.

(CHAIRPERSON Start closing at 5 minutes before the end of the meeting.)

CLOSING THE MEETING

That's all the time we have for sharing tonight. Thank you all for sharing. We have no dues or fees, but are fully self-supporting through our own contributions. In keeping with our 7th Tradition, we will pass a basket to help with group expenses.

- Are there any announcements?
- Are there any anniversaries this month?
- Are there any newcomers?

We suggest that you attend this meeting for a complete cycle of 14 consecutive weeks. If that sounds like a lot, then just make this meeting once a week, and the 14 will take care of itself.

In closing: what we hear at this meeting should remain at the meeting. Please respect the anonymity and confidences of those who have shared tonight.

Would someone please read The ACA Promises? (p. 176). If using the *ACA Fellowship Text (BRB)*, The ACA Promises can be found on p. 591.

Thanks. We close the meeting with ACA Serenity Prayer (p. 176). If using the *ACA Fellowship Text (BRB)*, The ACA Serenity Prayer can be found on p. 424.

KEEP COMING BACK!

Appendix C

The Laundry List – Problem
(From The ACA Fellowship Text Chapter 1)[5]

*A*CA cofounder Tony A. wrote the 14 Traits of an adult child of an alcoholic in 1978. When read in New York at the first ACA group, an adult child said: "Oh boy, that's my laundry list!" Since that time, the 14 Traits have been referred to as The "Laundry List."

From the descriptive power of the traits, ACA was born and created. In just 260 words, The Laundry List describes the thinking and personality of an adult reared in a dysfunctional family. A sample of the 14 Traits reveals how we judge ourselves and others harshly. We remain in destructive or loveless relationships because we fear abandonment.

The term "adult child" means that we respond to adult interactions with fear and self-doubt learned as children. This undercurrent of hidden fear can sabotage our choices and relationships. We can appear outwardly confident while living with a constant question of our worth.

In ACA, we believe the experiences of growing up in a dysfunctional family affect us as adults. Many of us have had successful careers but still felt disconnected from life. Some of us have experienced regular failure. We lived with a self-created calamity mixed with self-harm and self-hate. Many of us have been in the middle of success and failure. We have had fine jobs and homes, but we wondered why others appeared to be enjoying life while we guessed at what was normal. We felt like we were on the outside looking in. Whatever our path, we found no lasting help until we found ACA.

Since its first writing, The Laundry List has been adapted by various groups and authors. West Coast ACA groups placed The Laundry List in a narrative form known as The Problem, which is read at the beginning of ACA meetings throughout the fellowship. The Laundry List traits are also known as the common behavior characteristics among many ACA members.

In this chapter, we offer the original Laundry List as written by our primary founder. We are not eliminating The Problem read at ACA meetings. The 14 Traits are part of ACA's foundational language that creates identity among ACA's varied membership. Adult children who are codependents, drug addicts, food addicts, gamblers, sex addicts, and workaholics relate equally to the personality traits of The Laundry List. It is not uncommon for an adult child to be acting out in one or more addictions or compulsions at the same time. This "addictiveness" is our nature as adult children.

---

5 Adult Children of Alcoholics, *ACA Fellowship Text,* excerpt from pp. 3-4, 8-9, and 10-18, Signal Hill: ACA WSO, 2006

Additionally, The Laundry List attracts adult children from families in which addiction was not an issue. Some of these families include parents who were emotionally ill, hypochondriac, hypercritical, perfectionistic, ultra-religious, or sexually abusive. Adults who have been adopted or who grew up in foster homes relate to The Laundry List as well and recover in ACA.

Many members say The Laundry List is a powerful piece of literature that raised the veil of denial they had lived under as adults. Scholarly studies have shown that many of the traits are specific to adult children. We believe the list is a gateway into a life of clarity and self-acceptance.

The "Other" Laundry List

Before we write in greater detail about the original Laundry List, we must note that most of the 14 Traits have an opposite. Our experience shows that the opposites are just as damaging as the counterpart. For example, if we feared authority figures, as the first trait suggests, we also became authority figures to our children, spouses, or others. When we stop and think about it, we realize we were feared as authority figures. If we lived our life from the viewpoint of a victim (Trait 5), then many of us have become persecutors or perpetrators who created victims. If we got guilt feelings for standing up for ourselves (Trait 7), we could also feel guiltless by shaming someone verbally. We could take from others what was not ours without feeling guilty.

These examples represent the reverse side of The Laundry List. Many of us would like to deny that we have been a dominating authority figure, but we have. We don't like to think about victimizing others or projecting blame onto them, but we have. Many of us have reenacted what was done to us, thinking we were justified. Some of us have engaged in fights that go beyond mere words. We have slapped and slugged others in a fit of rage. Some of us have used a violent cursing with threats of physical harm to intimidate others. A few adult children have willingly committed crimes. We have stolen merchandise, written bogus checks, or embezzled money for various reasons that don't hold weight in the light of our explanations. We can feel shame or disgust when we think about our actions. This is healthy guilt, which is different from the toxic guilt that we were raised under.

Our behaviors, whether we are a victim or creating victims, highlight an ACA truism: "ACA is not an easy program to work." Yet, the effort it takes to work ACA is far less than the effort it takes to live in codependence or trying to control others or circumstances out of our control. If we apply half the effort to ACA that we apply to living codependently, we will see amazing results. We will find clarity and self-worth.

We will need help. We will need acceptance from others when we cannot accept ourselves. We do not need to shame ourselves or dive into self-condemnation, but we must be honest about our behavior. We sometimes need a reminder that we are acting destructively and should consider rethinking our behavior.

ACA allows us to admit our behaviors in a safe place without judgment from others. By working the ACA program, we learn to recognize when we are thinking like a victim or persecutor and to talk about it. We reparent ourselves with gentleness and self-love. We become open-minded to the idea that we can change with time and with help.

Reviewing The Laundry List

Trait 1:   We become isolated and afraid of people and authority figures.

Adult children often live a secret life of fear. Fear, or sometimes terror, is one of the connecting threads that link the 14 Traits together. Two of the first three traits describe our fear of people. While many adult children appear cheerful, helpful, or self sufficient, most live in fear of their parents and spouses in addition to fearing an employer. Others are constantly afraid of failing finances, imagined health problems, or world disasters. They have a sense of impending doom or that nothing seems to work out. Even the seemingly bold adult child who shows bravado can be covering up a deep sense of feeling unsafe or unlovable.

At the core of these thoughts is usually the fear of being shamed or abandoned. Shame is the deep sense that our souls are inherently flawed. Abandonment means more than being left alone or left at a doorstep.

Shame and abandonment are two of the most identifiable traits of a dysfunctional home. Among other factors, they are two of the conditions that help produce an adult child whether alcohol or drugs are in the home or not. Adult children from all family types not only feel shame deeply, but we believe we are shame. In some cases, adult-child shame is so pervasive that it can paralyze the person's body and mind. Adult children have described "shame attacks," which can cause physical illness or an age regression. During age regression, an adult child can feel physically small. Even vision can be affected when shame is released into the body. An intense shame episode can cause room dimensions to appear warped and lighting to appear odd. Many adult children have difficulty fully breathing during these moments.

Abandonment can take many forms. One form is as simple as the parent leaving the child alone without returning. Or it can involve parental perfectionism in which a child's behavior never measures up. Parents abandon their children when they fail to praise or recognize a child's true effort to please the parent. Instead, most parents are quick to criticize and correct a child's behavior but rarely find time to praise the child or to build confidence for good choices. As a result, most adult children have a critical parent inside. The critical, inner parent berates or undermines the person at almost every turn. This critical inner parent is a form of self-abandonment.

Shame and abandonment. That is how our dysfunctional families controlled us as children. We came to see our parents as authority figures who could not be trusted.

We transfer that fear to our adult lives, and we fear our employers, certain relatives, and group situations. We fear authority figures or become an authority figure.

Trait 2:   *We become approval seekers and lost our identity in the process.*

Trait 3:   *We are frightened by angry people and any personal criticism.*

Becoming a people pleaser is one of the solutions that adult children apply to avoid being criticized, shamed, or abandoned. Adult children also attempt to disarm angry or frightening people with approval seeking behavior. We give up some of our identity when we engage in such behavior. We believe that we will be safe and never abandoned if we are "nice" and if we never show anger. However, being a people-pleaser comes with a heavy price. When we please others at the expense of our feelings or needs, we invariably end up hurting ourselves and our relationships. Many adult children vacillate between being sugary sweet and explosively angry. They often explode, feel deep remorse, and promise to change only to repeat the cycle. Many adult children swallow their anger only to produce cases of depression or panic attacks. Whether explosively angry or routinely sorrowful, these behaviors are a vicious cycle that harms our relationships.

At the core, people-pleasing is dishonest and creates the wrong foundation for a meaningful relationship that most adult children really want deep down inside.

Many adult children constantly survey their homes or relationships, looking for situations that could lead to shame or some other public act of criticism. In addition to fearing shame and abandonment, our hyper-vigilance is intensified by what many therapists call Post-Traumatic Stress Disorder. PTSD is most often associated with combat veterans or survivors of a traumatic event such as a car wreck or a catastrophic event. However, adult children suffer from PTSD as well. A PTSD event or events produce such a high state of threat or danger that experts believe it changes the body chemistry. Long after the threat has passed, the PTSD sufferer remains on "alert" to ward off future events that could retrigger the fear of the previous fearful event.

Trait 4:   *We either become alcoholics, marry them or both, or find another compulsive personality such as a workaholic to fulfill our sick abandonment needs.*

Trait 9:   *We confuse love with pity and tend to "love" people we can "pity" and "rescue."*

Trait 13:   *Alcoholism is a family disease and we became para-alcoholics and took on the characteristics of that disease even though we did not pick up the drink.*

Since alcoholism is a family disease, all family members are affected without having to take a drink. With an amazing predictability, the children grow up to be addicted or marry an addicted or compulsive person. Many adult children become addicted to alcohol or other drugs, thinking their lives will be different than their parents. However, an addicted adult child often surpasses the parents' dysfunctional behavior in drug use and actions. ACA works best for those abstaining from alcohol, drugs, and prescription medication. We cannot work an effective program if we are dosing ourselves with alcohol or drugs. At the same time, ACA members should consult their doctor before making a decision to abstain from medication. This is a decision you should make with your doctor.

Adult children intuitively link up with other adult children in relationships and social settings. As bizarre as it sounds, many adult children are attracted to an abusive, addicted person because that person resembles an addictive or abusive parent. Before recovery, many adult children tend to choose people who will abandon them so they can feel the familiar pain of being unwanted. We can also switch from feeling like a victim to reacting like a persecutor.

Because we confuse love with pity and have an over-developed sense of responsibility, our abusive relationships "fit" with a subconscious set of traits we are looking for in a mate or significant other. While many adult children would protest that they would not choose such a person, they are actually left without a choice until they get help in ACA. Before recovery, if the adult child manages to leave their unhappy relationship, the person usually selects the same type of abandoning and abusive person in the next relationship. Without help, we are doomed to seek out people who treat us as we were treated as children. Traits 4, 9, and 13 are a factor in these decisions.

Trait 5: *We live life from the viewpoint of victims, and we are attracted by that weakness in our love and friendship relationships.*

Trait 6: *We have an overdeveloped sense of responsibility, and it is easier for us to be concerned with others rather than ourselves. This enables us not to look too closely at our own faults.*

Our experience shows that we often lived as victims. By living as victims or with victim characteristics, adult children seek to control others and ward off potentially shaming or abandoning situations. Taking the victim position can be shrewdly manipulative for an adult child who knows how to use it; however, being a victim loses its power when overused. People tire of such behavior and tend to move on. This causes the adult child to select another victim to reenact the behavior. Many adult children, who practice being a victim, often switch over to the super-responsible role in preparation for a return to the victim role. By taking on too much work and responsibility, the person can vault into a fit of rage, collapse, or isolation. The person hopes to garner sympathy and pity. The victim reemerges.

Playing the victim or being overly responsible allows the adult child to avoid focusing on himself or herself. Both roles are saturated with codependent avoidance of feelings and being responsible for one's own feelings. By concerning ourselves with others and their chaos, we avoid doing anything about our own lives. By being overly concerned about others, adult children wrongly think they are involved in life. In reality, they are missing life. The enmeshed, codependent ACA can be so wrapped up in another person's thoughts and actions that the adult child has no inner life or outer support when the relationship wanes. Codependent ACAs describe feeling lethargic, disoriented, and hopeless when their partners are gone. This is the high price for focusing on others.

Trait 7: ***We get guilt feelings when we stand up for ourselves instead of giving in to others.***

Trait 11: ***We judge ourselves harshly and have a very low sense of self-esteem.***

Who could have his home burglarized and feel like he or she did something wrong? An adult child.

Who could feel guilty about asking a cashier to correct a mistake when the cashier handed back incorrect change? An adult child.

Before recovery, most adult children assume they are wrong whatever the situation might be. If a mistake is made on the job, the adult child takes responsibility for it. If someone feels upset, we think we might have done something to cause the feelings in another. On the flip side we can blame others and avoid taking responsibility for our errors or poor behavior. We can judge ourselves harshly and place blame on ourselves and others willingly when such blame is not necessary.

Because of our shaming childhoods, adult children doubt and blame themselves in a knee-jerk reaction that is predictable and consistent yet rarely observed until recovery is encountered. We react instead of thinking about options and then acting.

The guilty feelings we encounter when standing up for ourselves have their roots in not being allowed to ask for what we needed as children. Judging ourselves harshly comes from abusive and hypercritical parents. As children, we went without basic needs or praise. We were vulnerable children, but we were shamed when we expressed a legitimate need. "You are so selfish," our parents said. "Do you ever think of anyone else but yourself? Do you think I am made of money?"

As adults, we remember such interactions with our parents. We refeel the pain of being dismissed or shamed when speaking up for a want or need. As adults, many of us avoid asking for what we need to avoid old pain. Others manipulate to get what they think they want. They are unhappy a lot. Even when we get what we think we want, we realize it is not enough again.

Trait 8: ***We become addicted to excitement.***

When ACA founder Tony A. wrote this trait, he originally stated: "We become addicted to fear" but changed the wording to "addicted to excitement" for clarity. Either way – excitement or fear – adult children use both to mimic the feeling of being alive when in reality they are recreating a scene from their family of origin. Gossip, dramatic scenes, pending financial failure, or failing health are often the turmoil that adult children create in their lives to feel connected to reality. While such behavior is rarely stated as such, these behaviors are an "addiction" to excitement or fear.

Because we were raised in chaotic or controlling homes, our internal compass is oriented toward excitement, pain, and shame. This inner world can be described as an "inside drug store." The shelves are stocked with bottles of excitement, toxic shame, self hate, self -doubt, and stress. Other shelves include canisters of lust, fear, and worry. As odd as it sounds, we can seek out situations so we can experience a "hit" of one of these inner drugs. We can create chaos to feel excitement. Or we procrastinate on the job to feel stress. Before finding ACA, we picked relationships that triggered our childhood unrest because it felt normal to be upset, persecuted, or shamed. During these moments, we thought we felt alive with excitement, but in reality we were staying just ahead of our aching childhood. Our actions as adults represent our addiction to excitement and a variety of inner drugs created to survive childhood. Many of our repressed feelings have actually been changed into inner drugs that drive us to harm ourselves or others. Without help, we cannot recognize serenity or true safety. Because our homes were never consistently safe or settled, we have no true reference point for these states of being. Without ACA, we can view emotionally healthy people as boring or confusing.

Trait 10: ***We have "stuffed" our feelings from our traumatic childhoods and have lost the ability to feel or express our feelings because it hurts so much (Denial).***

Trait 10 highlights the body feature of the disease of family dysfunction. The ACA disease model addresses the body, mind, and spirit of the adult child. Clinical research strongly suggests that childhood trauma or neglect are stored in the tissue of the children. The emotional or physical trauma does not go away without an effort to address the original cause. In some cases the stored hurt creates a dissociative effect in the adult. The adult child has dissociated from his or her body. The person appears to function quite normally in society; however, the stored trauma is there, creating bodily ailments that can appear as depression, panic disorders, hyperactivity, or sloth. Because of this storing or dissociation, many adult children are truly baffled when a counselor suggests the person is holding down feelings or avoiding feelings.

Trait 12: ***We are dependent personalities who are terrified of abandonment and will do anything to hold on to a relationship in order not to experience painful abandonment feelings which we received from living with sick people who were never there emotionally for us.***

Trait 14: ***Para-alcoholics (codependents) are reactors rather than actors.***

Adult children are dependent personalities, who view abuse and inappropriate behavior as normal. Or if they complain about the abuse, they feel powerless to do anything about it. Without help, adult children confuse love and pity and pick partners they can pity and rescue. The payoff is a feeling of being needed or avoiding feeling alone for another day. Such relationships create reactors, who feel powerless to change their situations. They freely use the 14 Traits of an adult child to negotiate for crumbs of attention. Others use the traits to create smothering over-dependence by their partners. Until they find recovery, they lack the language and support needed to recognize the problem. A proven solution awaits in ACA.

Appendix D
Traits Tables

TRAIT 1

The Laundry List	The Other Laundry List
We became isolated and afraid of people and authority figures.	To cover our fear of people and our dread of isolation we tragically become the very authority figures who frighten others and cause them to withdraw.
The Flip Side of The Laundry List	**The Flip Side of The Other Laundry List**
We move out of isolation and are not unrealistically afraid of other people, even authority figures.	We face and resolve our fear of people and our dread of isolation and stop intimidating others with our power and position.

TRAIT 2

The Laundry List	The Other Laundry List
We became approval seekers and lost our identity in the process.	To avoid becoming enmeshed and entangled with other people and losing ourselves in the process, we become rigidly self-sufficient. We disdain the approval of others.
The Flip Side of The Laundry List	**The Flip Side of The Other Laundry List**
We do not depend on others to tell us who we are.	We realize the sanctuary we have built to protect the frightened and injured child within has become a prison and we become willing to risk moving out of isolation.

TRAIT 3

The Laundry List	The Other Laundry List
We are frightened by angry people and any personal criticism.	*We frighten people with our anger and threat of belittling criticism.*
The Flip Side of The Laundry List	**The Flip Side of The Other Laundry List**
We are not automatically frightened by angry people and no longer regard personal criticism as a threat.	*With our renewed sense of self-worth and self-esteem we realize it is no longer necessary to protect ourselves by intimidating others with contempt, ridicule and anger.*

TRAIT 4

The Laundry List	The Other Laundry List
We either become alcoholics, marry them, or both, or find another compulsive personality such as a workaholic to fulfill our sick abandonment needs.	*We dominate others and abandon them before they can abandon us or we avoid relationships with dependent people altogether. To avoid being hurt, we isolate and dissociate and thereby abandon ourselves.*
The Flip Side of The Laundry List	**The Flip Side of The Other Laundry List**
We do not have a compulsive need to recreate abandonment.	*We accept and comfort the isolated and hurt inner child we have abandoned and disavowed and thereby end the need to act out our fears of enmeshment and abandonment with other people.*

TRAIT 5

The Laundry List	The Other Laundry List
We live life from the viewpoint of victims and we are attracted by that weakness in our love and friendship relationships.	*We live life from the standpoint of a victimizer, and are attracted to people we can manipulate and control in our important relationships.*
The Flip Side of The Laundry List	**The Flip Side of The Other Laundry List**
We stop living life from the standpoint of victims and are not attracted by this trait in our important relationships.	*Because we are whole and complete we no longer try to control others through manipulation and force and bind them to us with fear in order to avoid feeling isolated and alone.*

TRAIT 6

The Laundry List	The Other Laundry List
We have an overdeveloped sense of responsibility and it is easier* for us to be concerned with others rather than ourselves. This enables us not to look too closely at our own faults.	*We are irresponsible and self-centered. Our inflated sense of self-worth and self-importance prevents us from seeing our deficiencies and shortcomings.*
The Flip Side of The Laundry List	**The Flip Side of The Other Laundry List**
We do not use enabling as a way to avoid looking at our own shortcomings.	*Through our in-depth inventory we discover our true identity as capable, worthwhile people. By asking to have our shortcomings removed we are freed from the burden of inferiority and grandiosity.*

TRAIT 7

The Laundry List	The Other Laundry List
We get guilt feelings when we stand up for ourselves instead of giving in to others.	*We make others feel guilty when they attempt to assert themselves.*
The Flip Side of The Laundry List	**The Flip Side of The Other Laundry List**
We do not feel guilty when we stand up for ourselves.	*We support and encourage others in their efforts to be assertive.*

TRAIT 8

The Laundry List	The Other Laundry List
We become addicted to excitement.	*We inhibit our fear by staying deadened and numb.*
The Flip Side of The Laundry List	**The Flip Side of The Other Laundry List**
We avoid emotional intoxication and choose workable relationships instead of constant upset.	*We uncover, acknowledge and express our childhood fears and withdraw from emotional intoxication.*

TRAIT 9

The Laundry List	The Other Laundry List
We confuse love with pity and tend to "love" people who we can "pity" and "rescue".	*We hate people who "play" the victim and beg to be rescued.*
The Flip Side of The Laundry List	**The Flip Side of The Other Laundry List**
We are able to distinguish love from pity, and do not think "rescuing" people we "pity" is an act of love.	*We have compassion for anyone who is trapped in the "drama triangle" and is desperately searching for a way out of insanity.*

TRAIT 10

The Laundry List	The Other Laundry List
We have stuffed our feelings from our traumatic childhoods and have lost the ability to feel or express our feelings because it hurts so much (denial).	*We deny that we've been hurt and are suppressing our emotions by the dramatic expression of "pseudo" feelings.*
The Flip Side of The Laundry List	**The Flip Side of The Other Laundry List**
We come out of denial about our traumatic childhoods and regain the ability to feel and express our emotions.	*We accept we were traumatized in childhood and lost the ability to feel. Using the 12 Steps as a program of recovery we regain the ability to feel and remember and become whole human beings who are happy, joyous and free.*

TRAIT 11

The Laundry List	The Other Laundry List
We judge ourselves harshly and have a very low sense of self-esteem.	*To protect ourselves from self punishment for failing to "save" the family we project our self-hate onto others and punish them instead.*
The Flip Side of The Laundry List	**The Flip Side of The Other Laundry List**
We stop judging and condemning ourselves and discover a sense of self-worth.	*In accepting we were powerless as children to "save" our family we are able to release our self-hate and to stop punishing ourselves and others for not being enough.*

TRAIT 12

The Laundry List	The Other Laundry List
We are dependent personalities who are terrified of abandonment and will do anything to hold on to a relationship in order not to experience painful abandonment feelings which we received from living with sick people who were never there emotionally for us.	*We "manage" the massive amount of deprivation we feel, coming from abandonment within the home, by quickly letting go of relationships that threaten our "independence" (not too close).*
The Flip Side of The Laundry List	**The Flip Side of The Other Laundry List**
We grow in independence and are no longer terrified of abandonment. We have interdependent relationships with healthy people, not dependent relationships with people who are emotionally unavailable.	*By accepting and reuniting with the inner child we are no longer threatened by intimacy, by the fear of being engulfed or made invisible.*

TRAIT 13

The Laundry List	The Other Laundry List
Alcoholism is a family disease and we became para-alcoholics and took on the characteristics of the disease even though we did not pick up the drink.	*We refuse to admit we've been affected by family dysfunction or that there was dysfunction in the home or that we have internalized any of the family's destructive attitudes and behaviors.*
The Flip Side of The Laundry List	**The Flip Side of The Other Laundry List**
The characteristics of alcoholism and para-alcoholism we have internalized are identified, acknowledged, and removed.	*By acknowledging the reality of family dysfunction we no longer have to act as if nothing were wrong or keep denying that we are still unconsciously reacting to childhood harm and injury.*

TRAIT 14

The Laundry List	The Other Laundry List
Para-alcoholics are reactors rather than actors.	*We act as if we are nothing like the dependent people who raised us.*
The Flip Side of The Laundry List	**The Flip Side of The Other Laundry List**
We are actors, not reactors.	*We stop denying and do something about our post-traumatic dependency on substances, people, places and things to distort and avoid reality.*

Appendix E

Awareness vs. Consciousness

In *Primal Man: The New Consciousness*[6], Art Janov and Michael Holden distinguished the difference between being *aware* and being *conscious*.

Awareness

When content is unrelated and only symbolically derived from the subconscious, there is only awareness.

In other words, when we are busy with our daily lives – our circumstances, situations, the job or the lack of a job, our significant other, the lack of a significant other, money, the lack of money, illness, the lives of our friends and loved ones, etc. – and are not *conscious* of why things are the way they are, we are not really grounded, we are only **aware**.

Consciousness

When content is directly related to subconscious processes, there is consciousness.

When we are in touch with **who and why** things are the way they are, **what and how** we set it up, **where** we learned the behavior and the attitudes that lead us to set up our lives in this way, we are grounded in *consciousness*.

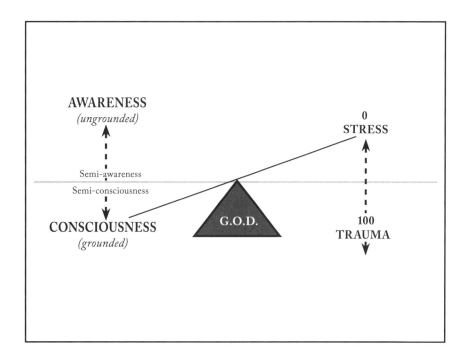

---

6 Janov, Arthur and Holden, E. Michael, *Primal Man: The New Consciousness*, New York: Thomas Y. Crowell Company, 1975

The ACA Promises

1) We will discover our real identities by loving and accepting ourselves.

2) Our self-esteem will increase as we give ourselves approval on a daily basis.

3) Fear of authority figures and the need to "people-please" will leave us.

4) Our ability to share intimacy will grow inside us.

5) As we face our abandonment issues, we will be attracted by strengths and become more tolerant of weaknesses.

6) We will enjoy feeling stable, peaceful, and financially secure.

7) We will learn how to play and have fun in our lives.

8) We will choose to love people who can love and be responsible for themselves.

9) Healthy boundaries and limits will become easier for us to set.

10) Fears of failure and success will leave us, as we intuitively make healthier choices.

11) With help from our ACA support group, we will slowly release our dysfunctional behaviors.

12) Gradually, with our Higher Power's help, we will learn to expect the best and get it.

The ACA Serenity Prayer

God, grant me the serenity

to accept the people I can not change,

the courage to change the one I can,

and the wisdom to know that one is me.

Notes

Notes

Notes

Notes